Moore - 2.16

A Sort of a Saga

By the Same Author

UP FRONT

BACK HOME

A Sort of a Saga

TEXT AND ILLUSTRATIONS

by Bill Mauldin

WILLIAM SLOANE ASSOCIATES

PUBLISHERS NEW YORK, N. Y.

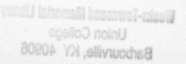

For NATALIE

A Sort of a Saga

Part One

R ECENTLY THE FAMILY DOCTOR BRACED
me against a fluoroscope, gasped in horror, said my lungs
looked like the inside of a Pittsburgh mill flue, and asked
how much I smoke.

"Two packs a day," I told him, and then added hastily,
"I don't really smoke that much because I work hard
all day over typewriters and drawing boards and have a
way of lighting a cigarette, taking a couple of drags, then
putting it down and forgetting about it." A double lie. I
don't work hard all day and I smoke cigarettes right down
to where they burn my fingers.

"Why don't you quit?" he asked. "You're young; you
won't miss it after a week or two. How long have you had
the habit?"

I told him that I began life, so far as my memory is concerned, with a cigarette in my hand.

"My first recollection of this world," I said, "is of sitting on the bank of a little river in Parral, Chihuahua, Mexico, in 1924, at the age of three, finishing the last of a pack of Chesterfields which, according to three witnesses, I'd smoked in a little more than an hour."

As luck would have it, just then I happened to emit a hoarse cough, the first I'd had in weeks. The doctor backed hastily around his desk, putting six feet between us, and in a gentle tone he probably reserves for dying patients (I've learned since that he's a fanatic about smoking—advises all his customers to quit) he told me he'd like to hear the whole story.

My father, Sidney Mauldin, and his brother-in-law, George Bemis, were working together at a mine in Parral; my brother Sidney Jr. and I spent a great deal of time playing at Uncle George's house with his two sons, who were about our age. Sid was my senior by a year; I've had to reconstruct the first part of the smoking episode from his account. Uncle George had hidden a carton of smokes in his bureau drawer; we four kids had found it and toddled with it to the riverbank a short distance behind the house, and started smoking chain-fashion, having set out with only one match and being afraid to go back for more.

What must have jarred my memory into functioning, as it has been shakily ever since, was the scream of Uncle George's hefty and evil-tempered Mexican maid, who looked out the back door and saw us making clouds of smoke. The rest is vivid. She rushed at us, yelling and waving a mop, and we took to the river. We later figured, probably correctly, that she was sore only because we'd swiped smokes she'd planned to liberate for herself.

The wide, sluggish stream averaged about two feet in depth, which put the water right up to our chins. Every time one of us would step into a depression he'd go under. All kinds of things float along a slow Mexican river. Once my brother disappeared and came up wearing a crown of soggy tissue paper. The four of us made the far bank and looked back to see what the enemy was doing.

We instantly regretted having left the cigarettes scattered behind. The maid had picked them up and cached them about her person, and as we watched she brought a match out of her apron, struck it with her thumbnail, and sat down to wait for us, smoking calmly, the mop within easy reach. There was no way of escaping her without going far up or down river to cross back; we had just enough sense to realize that we might hit deep water or bad currents elsewhere. So we sat drying ourselves and wondering what to do. We all had a mastery of Spanish profanity remarkable for tots so small. One of us yelled *"Cabrón!"* at the enemy; promptly we all took it up as a chant, adding other choice words for a melody.

The *cabrón* stuff was a mistake. The maid glowered hideously at us, heaved to her feet, hitched her skirt up with one hand, grasped the mop with the other, and started to wade across, a cigarette stuck grimly in the corner of her mouth. We were pretty scared and were about to start upriver and take our chances with the water, when Uncle George showed up. He spoke with the maid for a moment —we couldn't hear what was said, but her mop was waving and she pointed several times at us.

After taking all the cigarettes away from her and putting

them into his pockets, Uncle George took off his shoes, rolled up his pants, and came after us, carrying us back two at a time. He sent Sid and me home for disciplining (my

memory fades conveniently here—I don't remember the penalty) and that was the end of the episode. But I have smoked at every opportunity since then. I wasn't sick from that first pack of cigarettes, nor was I ever sick from tobacco, not even after my first cigar at the age of six.

Of course, my folks did not approve of children smoking. But I became a master of subterfuge: I learned how to extract a cigarette or two from my Pop's pack so he wouldn't miss them, how to kill "smoker's breath," and how, when I hadn't had a chance to kill it, to hold my breath when kissing my parents good night. Until I be-

came old enough to smoke openly, some fifteen years later, I took full advantage of toothpaste's cleansing qualities; on successful days when I'd swiped several cigarettes and bummed more from amused citizens on Parral's street corners, I brushed my teeth as many as ten times.

"And so," I concluded to the doctor, who had listened patiently through all this, "even if *you* find my lungs foggy, I've heard a lot of dentists marvel at the fine condition of my teeth."

· 15 ·

He sent me on my way, no doubt expecting me to drop dead on the sidewalk outside, and I went home, still thinking about Mexico.

My golden age of smoking in Parral came when a regiment of the Mexican army was garrisoned in town for a while. The soldiers were poorly paid, but they could always be shaken down for one of those long, sweet-tasting, brown-paper cigarettes made down there. I considered them greatly superior to American brands. My brother never helped me raid the Mexican army. His stomach had become upset from the riverbank orgy, and he didn't start smoking until some time later. He missed a great deal, for the soldiers were fun. Each man carried several bandoleers over his shoulders. They didn't have enough cartridges to fill even one bandoleer, but a soldier would distribute a handful of shiny brass shells all around his person, leaving many empty loops, so it always looked as if he'd just been through a very fierce action. The regiment had several antique artillery pieces, which were impressive but probably very dangerous to shoot.

I became friendly with two bushy-faced noncoms who must have been the most heavily armed soldiers in military history. Each had two pistols, a huge knife, a bayonet, a rifle, and a vast assortment of bandoleers. They carried their arsenals everywhere. One day I saw them walking up the street past our house, and ran out to catch up with them. They were walking pretty fast; they didn't seem to hear me call them, and I couldn't catch up with them, so I trailed along a couple of hundred yards behind, meaning to overtake them when they stopped. They finally turned up a side street and went in the front door of a large house on the outskirts of town. When I got to the door they'd disappeared inside. Nobody answered my knock, so I went around back, where I found three fat ladies making tortillas on the flat top of the big kitchen stove.

" 'Allo, keed," they greeted me cheerfully. "Wot's you name?"

"Beellee," I said, determined to show my Spanish was just as good as theirs.

"Beellee," they repeated, enunciating carefully. " 'Ave a tortilla, Beellee." It was thin, delicious, and very hot. They gave me several more, rolling them around in a fine hot sauce and salting the outside. I forgot my soldiers and spent the whole afternoon with the ladies. The place turned out to be full of fat ladies. They were all jolly with the little gringo and they all made good tortillas. From time to time one or two would leave the kitchen, I could hear male and female voices in the front of the house, and then many feet would clump up the stairs. And two or three new ladies would come in, grin toothily, and coo " 'Allo, Beellee!" at me.

I went back again the next day and thereafter every time I could get away from our house. Although my mother was a chronic worrier about her brood, there wasn't much trouble a kid could get into around Parral, and she was pretty liberal about letting us run around, always warning us to "Look out for cars, stay away from railroad tracks and the mine, and keep on the other side of the street from lepers and beggars." It was a small town and no matter where we went there was sure to be somebody who recognized us.

I don't know who noticed that I was becoming the mascot of Parral's leading bordello, but one day I was sitting in its kitchen when one of the fat ladies said, "Hey Beellee, here come you Papa."

"Naw," I said, not thinking to ask how she knew my father.

"Si, Beellee, you Papa coming. Look."

I poked my head around the kitchen door and sure enough it was Pop, coming into the back yard, ducking under a clothesline full of underwear, with a bad look on his face. His eyes were protruding and he seemed to be muttering something.

"*Cabrón*," I said.

"BEELLEE!" all three of them squealed at once. "That's no way talk about you Papa!"

"*Cabrón!*" I repeated just as the paternal form filled the doorway. Casting a dark glare at the tittering girls (I'm sure he thought they'd taught me the awful word), Pop yanked me out and away, dragging me home at such a clip my feet hardly touched the ground. It was foolish of him, actually, for never did the girls say or do anything unladylike in my presence. And they never would let me smoke when I was at their house. Had I remained with them a while longer I might have been cured of the vice.

The mining job in Parral, which lasted a year, was only one of Pop's many careers. He was not a person to stagnate in one place or one job for long. A rather tall, wiry, swarthy man with a fierce beak and a black mustache, he felt certain that somewhere in the world was a career which would make full use of his talents. He intended to find it if he had to hunt all his life.

Pop had grown up on his father's fruit farm in New Mexico, had decided bigger things than apples were in store for him, and had taken a correspondence course in electrical engineering, at that time a fairly new profession. Hardly had he finished, with high marks, when he decided he was more interested in autos and motorcycles. That was in Barney Oldfield's heyday. Pop found he had a tremendous flair for engines, and he played with the idea of becoming a racing driver. Helling up and down the Sacramento Mountains in New Mexico, he scared the daylights out of people and horses with his cars and motorcycles.

He might have taken up daredevil motoring permanently had the war not dragged him overseas, where he was gassed and generally banged up and given his fill of excitement. He came home, temporarily subdued, at the age of twenty-seven, married my mother, Katrina Bemis, who was sixteen, sired my brother and me in quick succession, worked for a while at farming, and then decided to try mining.

During the very early years of their marriage, my mother was easily carried away by Pop's oratory, and by the fun of chasing around with him on his careers, or "projects" as he sometimes called them. He had a deep, pleasant, rolling voice which was impossible to interrupt once it got started. He could talk, it seemed sometimes, on completely empty lungs.

When Pop was crossed or interrupted or questioned during a flight of oratory, he would tuck his head, which was normally rather handsome, deep into his slightly stooped shoulders, so that he had no neck at all—only a prominent Adam's apple which bobbed up and down furiously. His large ears would wiggle slightly; his wide, full mouth would draw into a straight, thin line and he would pull his lower lip between his teeth. His eyes would bulge and glare; the creases between them would deepen, and he would turn that remarkable countenance on whoever had defied him, whistling fiercely through his nose. This entire operation never lasted more than a second or two; his victim would retreat hastily and Pop would go on with his speech as if nothing had happened.

Pop didn't like
to be interrupted

If confronted with a really unruly audience, containing two or more chronic interrupters, a sentence of Pop's sometimes would go like this:

". . . So I says the fact that nobody's done it before doesn't mean it can't be done and he says it takes a lot of money for something like that huh [the "huh" was for air, a quick gasp which was part of the sentence and left no breach for anybody to jump in] well I says it seems to me that a man who depends on money and not his own hard work can't make a go of huh anything anyhow I don't give a damn he says you got to have money for something like that. . . ."

When he talked about a new scheme he went on for hours, painting a glorious picture and giving all the objections and then batting them down, as if six or seven people were discussing the matter instead of one. Sid and I never got over being entranced while Pop sold himself on something new. But as time went on my mother's eyes became less and less starry, and more and more often she would try to interrupt and "get a word in edgeways," as Pop described her effort. Finally, she got so she'd just sit and look on, slightly dazed, as he carried us away.

The gassing Pop got in the war had left him with a very wheezy variety of asthma. The affliction was genuine enough, but attacks always seemed to come with special fury at times when he felt a new project coming on, one which would carry him to a different climate. If we were in mountains and he felt the urge to try his luck in the plains, his asthma seemed suddenly aggravated by the high, thin air. When he began dreaming of hill country again, the thick, hot desert air threw him into spasms of wheezing. I've never doubted the severeness of his attacks, for I've seen him suffer badly; I have, however, often envied him for having an ailment which always cooperated with his plans.

He never tried politics; it was about the only career he missed, and I suspect now he would have been fine at it. He could filibuster better than anybody who ever sat in Congress. I don't know how he talked us down to Parral, but I do recall how he talked us away from there. Seems there was no future in the mining business, and he had a new project:

"All around the Southwest," he said, "there's thousands of people with wells and pumps and trucks and tractors and cars. They do their own repairs. They need wrenches. Man goes into a hardware store and says, 'Give me a wrench.' Just any old wrench. I says to myself [Pop always said "I says," or "He says"] these people need to get an appreciation of the difference between wrenches. There's a wrench for every purpose, I says, and sooner or later, they're going to find it out. Why shouldn't I be the man to tell them?"

He got very enthusiastic about the idea of selling things, for he knew he had a gift of gab, and if he could spiel and sway a customer as he did his family, he would have every rancher and farmer west of the Mississippi loaded with wrenches. So we pulled out of Parral and moved up to the border city of El Paso, Texas, where we rented a house.

While my mother sat home and wondered about Pop, and while Sid and I learned the art of infuriating streetcar conductors by putting marbles in the chinks where the lengths of track join (they crackle loudly under the wheels and make the conductor think he's broken something), Pop tore around the countryside in a brand-new Model T coupe with "Masterson, the Master of Wrenches" inscribed on the doors in gold leaf. It was the only new car we ever owned.

That was one of Pop's shortest-lived projects. The farmers didn't want progress. They continued to buy any old kind of wrench in hardware stores, but Pop had a wonderful time talking their arms off and he made many friends among them. In no time at all we bundled into the Model T, with "Masterson, the Master of Wrenches" still painted all over it, and with a huge collection of unsold wrenches in the back, we rolled north over the plains into New Mexico and chugged up the mountains to the ancestral fruit farm. Pop had decided to try apple-growing again.

Mountain Park, about seven thousand feet high in the Sacramento Mountains, is a fruit-growing community of several dozen families. Eighteen miles below, on the flat, dusty desert at the foot of the mountains, is Alamogordo, a sawmill town and the county seat, having two drugstores, a courthouse, a pool hall, a garage, and a very good weekly newspaper. (In the twenty years since the time I'm describing, Alamogordo has grown larger and has gained the dubious distinction of having been within a hundred miles of the world's first atom bomb explosion.)

Six miles and a couple of thousand feet above Mountain Park is Cloudcroft, a resort town surrounded by beautiful country that's cool in summer and bitterly cold in winter. Its thick pine forests have been rather badly cut up; they were the source of the lumber sawed in the Alamogordo mills. Cloudcroft used to claim (and perhaps still does) the highest golf course in the world. The upper bourgeoisie from El Paso kept cottages there and flocked to the golf course and the riding stables in summer, a few of them returning in winter for the good skiing.

Cloudcroft also claimed the world's steepest standard-gauge railroad, a line which hauled the logs to Alamogordo. Both the highway and the railroad passed through Mountain Park and its sister community, High Rolls, a mile below. The train stopped at both places to drop off the mail as it huffed up in the morning, and slowed to pick it up as it squealed down in the evening, with all its brakes locked and hot. Long trains had two locomotives—one alone easily could have hauled any number of the light, empty log cars uphill, but it took all the pressure two engines could cook up to make the brakes hold on the way down.

The country from Alamogordo at the foot of the range to Cloudcroft at the crest, and beyond, was mostly devoted to ranching and logging, with tourists as a sideline. Mountain Park and High Rolls were the only two places devoted entirely to fruit farming. From them, you could look down at the immense panorama of the lower slopes, where cattle nosed around hot, rocky mesquite hills for fodder, and across the great flat plain, where gusts of wind picked up red dust and danced it in whirlwinds. The plain separated our Sacramentos from the distant gray San Andres range. At the end of the San Andres are the weird Organ Mountains, whose spires and jagged outlines looked enough like a pipe organ to some fanciful explorer once to make him think of the name.

The plain itself is bisected by a spectacular white splotch which could be seen from our height thirty miles away: an oblong desert of pure white gypsum, forty miles long and fifteen wide. The dazzling gypsum, which has about the consistency of sugar, is one of the West's great tourist attractions. The wind moves it and piles it into immense drifts so that except for the glaring heat it is like snow at the South Pole. Even rabbits and snakes at the White Sands grow hides the color of milk. What they exist on nobody knows, for nothing grows in the huge expanse.

After looking at the plains awhile, you could turn the other way and see mountains like the French Alps towering above—where, in the winter, snow piled deep, and, in summer, livestock grazed in lush valleys between sheltering ridges; where deer and occasional bear made fine hunting; and where once in a great while you could hear the ghastly yowl of a mountain lion.

That country is really very handsome. There are two worlds very near each other, and Mountain Park is on the dividing line between them. In fact, our pasture, consisting of two skinny hills running parallel to the rest of the place, was covered on the lower end by scrub oak and piñon; the upper end was studded with tall, handsome pines. Even the rattlesnake line ends at Mountain Park. About half a mile below is the head of Box Canyon, a spectacular gorge which winds down to the plains. Rattlers are fairly common right up to our end of it, but not one has ever been found on our place.

A Mountain Park kid with imagination could travel a little way downhill and play at being a rangy plainsman, or he could go uphill and think of himself as a rugged, wiry mountaineer. Or he could stay where he was and think of himself as a fruit farmer, which was less glamorous but more lucrative. I always preferred the mountain stuff myself.

Besides apples, a lot of cherries and pears were raised at Mountain Park and High Rolls, and a few peaches and other fruits. Farming there paid off enough to keep people going; a few even got prosperous at it—but it is a tricky country. There are late spring or early fall frosts, and midsummer hailstorms. Orchards there are not for people who have to work on a shoestring; sometimes several years pass before a really good crop comes in.

Pop's father, a peppery little man who'd started punching cattle in Texas in the seventies, and worked as a scout for the army during the Geronimo wars in the eighties, had saved his money, looked around for a likely spot to settle down, and had started our Mountain Park place around the turn of the century. His full name is William Henry Mauldin; his cronies call him Uncle Billy. I was named after him.

When Pop came home from the war and got married, Uncle Billy, who had been a hard and steady worker with imagination and had made the farm a successful enterprise, turned the place over to his son. He retired with his wife to the lovely little village of La Luz, which sits like an oasis on the desert at the foot of the Sacramentos, ten miles from Mountain Park, on the road to Alamogordo.

Had Uncle Billy known his boy's ways a little better, he'd have stayed a while on the farm to break him in. Not long after Sid and I were born Pop had got restless and started off on the Parral project, leaving the farm rented. When we returned it was in terrible shape. The tenants, in what I suppose was a quite human way, had exploited the orchard, letting hired pickers climb all over the trees instead of using ladders, so that they skinned bark and broke branches. The tenants hadn't bothered about pruning or spraying. They'd let the fences fall down, the house go to pot, and weeds and brush grow all over everything.

"Goddam shiftless way to act huh I'll never trust human nature again look at all the work we got to do now!" Pop roared with indignation, this time and, with few exceptions, every other time we returned from "projects," having left the place rented.

But I suspect that in a way he enjoyed the challenge of a run-down place. I know that we only stayed on that farm when new trees needed planting, the house needed fixing, and land needed clearing. We never remained there once everything was in good shape and we could have relaxed and enjoyed the fruits (literally) of the hard work. Pop was bored with anything that didn't need fixing.

This attitude of his also applied to machines. Over the years we owned a succession of cars and trucks, trading one for another. Most were wrecks. Pop would overhaul each one and make it run better than it had when new, then he'd get tired of it and look for something else. Occasionally, when he had a vehicle he really liked, he would leave something loose in its ignition or fuel system, so there always would be a chance of breakdown on a lonely road in the middle of the night, preferably in a storm, and the machine would keep him interested and on his toes.

Pop was anything but lazy. He just needed a manager, that's all. Or a desert island. With his great energy and his ability to do anything with his hands he'd have made a marvelous Robinson Crusoe.

Sid showed very early that he'd inherited Pop's talents. Already he'd begun looking for things to take apart and put together. An old gentleman named Braunstein, who owned the farm adjacent to the western end of ours, once gave Sid and me several old pocket watches. Sid promptly took all his watches apart, then appropriated mine and took them apart too. He'd reconstruct timepieces from the pile of parts, and he was proud of the fact that he could dismantle two watches, reassemble them, and have enough parts left over to start making a third.

I, on the other hand, had no talents at all—not even a basic understanding of what made the world go around. For instance, I'd observed that on cold mornings Pop would take some kerosene out of one of the lamps, or the gallon can in the kitchen, and go around pouring the stuff on the blaze in the living room fireplace or the bedroom heater. Noting that the liquid was clear, I assumed it was water, and so one cold morning I took over the job, on my own initiative. I filled a stew-pan with water and made the rounds of the fires, putting them all out and filling the house so full of steam and smoke that we all had to go outside in the bitter cold, in our pajamas, until the air cleared. I remember my precocious brother consoling everybody.

"It's a good thing Billy didn't find the kerosene can or we wouldn't have no house left."

Sid and I were too young to be much help during the general repairs on the farm, but we were given a few little chores to do regularly. My principal job was bringing in stovewood—a simple task, since the wood was all cut and the woodbox had a convenient outside opening. All I had to do was carry four sticks (my limit) at a time, make about half a dozen trips, and the box was full. It was then that I began to learn the fine art of goldbricking, and to realize that farming was not for me. I would look into the box in the morning and, if it was low, make myself scarce for the day. My parents found it easier to fill the box themselves than spend time looking for me.

But I used to love tagging around after Pop and watching him work, especially when he was inventing something. Just as concert halls are filled with paying customers, most of whom have a hard time playing the piano with one finger, so I appreciated mechanical ability even though I lacked it.

The first big invention of Pop's which I was privileged

to witness was his spraying machine. The orchard needed treatment badly, but Pop hated to spend money for a sprayer when he felt he could make his own. Our "Masterson Wrench" Ford had been replaced by a dilapidated old truck. Taking me in the truck with him, Pop rattled around neighboring farms until he found the most essential part for his sprayer—an engine. It was an ancient, rusty, one-cylinder, two or three horsepower affair which had been propped against the back wall of a barn for years. Pop offered to buy it, but the owner gave it to us gladly, for, he said, it had been a clutter in his yard and he'd often wondered how to get rid of it.

With the donor's help Pop got the engine on the truck and we took it home. It was lovingly dismantled and every part was cleaned and greased.

Pop had a way of talking to anything he worked on.

"Come on, baby, come on. Get in there, you sonofa—" he would say to the intake valve, as he struggled with the spring. Then he would remember his youngest son standing there with wide, admiring eyes, and would finish lamely, "Get in there." Then he'd mutter and grunt happily for a while until he barked his fingers.

"Gahdamsonabitch. Hell. GET IN THERE!" He'd look guiltily around his shoulder at me, and I would pretend to have my mind elsewhere. And after a while he'd skin his hand again and I'd say "Gahdamsonabitch" for him.

"Listen, sprout," he'd say, "cut that out." But even from behind him, I could tell he was grinning, for his cheek would pull up to a point and his ears would shift. He almost always called Sid and me "sprout" or "whelp."

Muttering and puttering, Pop got the engine back together. It was no longer a corroded relic, but a gleaming, dripping work of art, standing proudly in its own grease. I was sent to the store-post office for the only part of the whole sprayer which ever required a cash outlay—a spark plug. Pop installed it, wound up the flywheel, and the old one-lung contraption exploded into life.

"WHOOSH, ha, ha, ha, WHOOSH, ha, ha, ha, ha, *BAM*, ha, ha, WHOOSH, ha ha!"

Pop had started it without securing its base; it danced joyfully about and threatened to take wing any moment. Yelling at it and circling it, looking for a hold, we grabbed it and wrestled it to a halt. Pop seized a wrench and laid it across the spark plug and the iron cylinder-head, shorting it out and getting a tremendous shock. He was not addicted to the coarser words, but I remember distinctly that this brought a violent four-letter expletive which, even in the excitement of the moment, I duly noted and filed for future reference. After going "ha-ha-haaa" in a surly way for a few seconds, the engine finally gasped and died.

Like all mechanical people, Pop collected junk in great quantities. No matter where he went, he always picked up odd wheels and rods and bits of metal and discarded auto frames and gears and whatnot, feeling sure that each bit would come in handy sometime. We had an immense pile of scrap iron in our back yard. Finding four wheels that matched, Pop fitted them to a wagon-bed, making a carriage for the spraying machine. With Sid's help he worried the old engine up to the bed, using an improvised hoist hung from a tree limb, bolted the engine down securely, and started it roaring again. Coaxing and wheedling and fussing, he "tuned" the thing as carefully as if it had

been a Rolls-Royce airplane motor, and when the WHOOSHES and HA's were more or less evenly spaced and the thing purred as well as a single cylinder can purr, Pop set out again in the truck, this time taking Sid as a companion, and searched for an air compressor.

They came back shortly with a compressor even more ancient and rusty than the engine had been. But it seemed fairly sound basically, it had a gauge that worked, and after it had been cleaned and greased and tested it turned out to be a good job. The junk pile yielded up a discarded hot-water boiler which had never been designed to hold air, but it had no leaks and it served the purpose. Pop mounted the compressor and the boiler on the wagon-bed. Then, accompanied by a great deal of colorful muttering, began the long and intricate task of hooking all the parts together.

It would take pages to describe the ingenious conglomeration of wooden rods, pieces of crankshaft, wires, pulleys, and gears. But when it was finished the engine worked the compressor, which fed air into the boiler, which stored it without blowing a single seam. Pop mounted two fifty-gallon oil barrels on the wagon-bed—which was now thoroughly cluttered—to hold the spray mixture, a poisonous soup with an arsenic base. Wooden beaters were installed in the barrels to keep the spray mixed, and were connected by rods to a piece of crankshaft belted to the flywheel of the already overloaded engine.

The whole job took about a week. When the sprayer was finished Pop hitched it to our two workhorses and dragged it off to the orchard for a testing. I was disappointed in that; had Pop worked another week he'd have made the machine self-propelling. But it was a wondrous device—it sprayed the trees thoroughly, and with such force it could have doubled as the local fire engine. Its creaking and groaning and banging scared the horses a little at first, but they got used to it.

Hardly had the trees been sprayed and the place generally fixed up, when Pop got restless. One day he cocked his eye across the narrow valley which separated our house from the post office, watched the streams of vacationers driving up the road to Cloudcroft, and began whistling gently and speculatively through his nose. As a log train chuffed up the mountain with two red and yellow excursion cars, packed with people, hooked onto its tail, Pop said to us:

"Why can't we sidetrack some of that business? There's no reason why Mountain Park couldn't be a tourist attraction. Hell, the only people who notice this place are the ones that stop at the store for gas. Look at Grace Rawlings' flowers. [She was a lady who had a large house and a fine flower garden in a little park behind the store.] Prettiest flowers in the country. People would come here in big crowds just to see those flowers, and there's lots of other attractions."

I think he even got my mother enthusiastic about this one. Spending all their money, they worked out elaborate plans and actually started building the first of several dozen cottages and eateries they planned to put all over our place.

All the odds were against it. The climate, for one thing. While cool breezes often blow down from higher places,

Mountain Park can get quite hot in summer, and stay that way for days. And though it often drops to zero in winter, and there are heavy snows, there could never be any winter sports because warm winds are always blowing up from the plains and melting the stuff or turning it into rain. Vacationers want extremes—either a warm winter for basking or a cold one for skiing; either a warm summer for swimming or a cool one for relaxing. Mountain Park could offer nothing but considerable mud during certain seasons, and a variable climate during others, when you risk sunstroke one day and freezing the next. Of course, Mountain Park had delicious apples for a stranger to chew while he marveled at the weird weather, but that was all.

Pop woke up to these facts about the same time he went broke. It was the last time he was ever able to afford a project on the grand scale.

Several houses at Mountain Park had plumbing, but ours had been one of the very first, and we were proud of it. Like everything else around the place, the plumbing generally needed overhauling after a tenancy, for some people didn't seem to appreciate a bathroom with a john that flushed, a lavatory that drained, a porcelain-lined bathtub, and hot and cold water. (After our return from one "project," we found that somebody had stored potatoes in the tub; the whole drain system had to be taken apart and de-potatoed.) Our water supply came from a tank several hundred yards above the house, on the side of a steep hill. It was fed by a little brook, and was so high above the house that we had tremendous pressure on our faucets.

The pipe which tapped the brook to feed the tank had a

screen over it, to keep out larger floating objects which might clog the pipe, or foul the tank, but in rainy weather or on irrigation days when some farmer above us piled clods into the stream to divert it for irrigation purposes, a lot of mud got into the tank. Pop had set the outlet pipe

high enough from the bottom of the tank so that two feet of mud could collect before our water would come down to the house dirty, and he cleaned it out periodically, but there was always some goo on the bottom.

Sid and I used to enjoy climbing into this tank when nobody was looking, and splashing around naked for hours at a time. Sooner or later somebody down at the house would turn on a faucet for a drink of water; when it came out so muddy it had to be chewed they would come up to the tank, fish us out, and paddle our tails. But since the creek was shallow and there was no other spot around for swimming, we felt the fun was worth the paddling.

My mother's parents lived on a hill overlooking the upper end of our place. I don't remember much about my grandfather Bemis except that he was held in awe because he'd known Mark Twain (in *Roughing It* Bemis is credited with killing a mule with one of those little gambler's derringers called a "Pepperbox"—no mean feat, since the weapon is not usually fatal to man at a distance greater than three feet). He paid me a penny a dozen for digging dandelions out of his lawn—all the roots had to come up and the grass had to be smoothed back—and once he almost pulled off my ear for saying "Darn" in front of him. His wife Callie, whom we called Nana, was (and still is) a chirpy little lady with great energy and a kind heart.

My mother's parents had been dead-set against her marriage to Pop. They thought she was too young and flighty. In fact, Uncle Billy and his wife thought so too. Each set of parents blamed the other for the marriage, although it was really nobody's doing but my folks', for they were both quite headstrong.

The result was that the Mauldins in La Luz and the Bemises in Mountain Park didn't have much to do with each other. But Sid and I enjoyed visiting all of them. Uncle Billy used to tell us fascinating stories about his youth as a cowpuncher and Indian fighter. He was one of the few old-timers who understated constantly. For example, once he told me how, when he had a farm for a while above

Cloudcroft and there was no civilization up there at all, he used to hunt deer for the family larder with a .45 single-action Colt pistol because he was saving his money and couldn't afford a rifle. I thought this a little hard to swallow until another old-timer told me he had not only seen my grandfather shoot a pistol as well as most experts could shoot a rifle, but that he could do it with either hand.

Uncle Billy

I remember listening once to an ex-deputy sheriff from Alamogordo tell my grandfather about a tough he'd arrested at gun point. Uncle Billy told him he was foolish to arrest a man that way.

"Son," he said, "don't ever pull your gun unless you're going to shoot, and don't ever shoot unless you're going to kill. Keep your gun in the scabbard. People know you mean business that way, and won't ever do anything to make you draw."

My grandfather had a fine Western-style wit. Once he was describing a big cattle drive from South Texas to

Dodge City, Kansas, in the '70s, when he worked as a cow-puncher. He mentioned bedding the cattle down one night, and a Virginia lady who was visiting asked him in perfect innocence what he meant by bedding down? He kept her on the hook for half an hour, describing in dead seriousness how they covered the beasts with quilts, and carried bundles of pillows to put under the heads of weak little calves. The lady took it all in and probably believes it to this day.

An old colored fellow named Brown lived on Uncle Billy's place. He was very stooped and feeble, and he did a few little chores like bringing in the wood every day. He'd been a slave in his childhood, and he was Sid's and my own private Uncle Remus. He was the only colored man either of us had ever seen, and he fascinated us. We asked him if he bled red like other people when he cut himself, and other such questions, and he was very patient and understanding with us. He, too, could tell wonderful stories, but his brain had become so feeble that he would start with one story and wind up with another, and we weren't too good an audience sometimes.

My grandfather thought a lot of Brown (whose first name I never learned; I don't think my grandfather knew it either; perhaps he had none) and there was no feeling of superiority or inferiority between the two old gentlemen. Uncle Billy had but one prejudice, and that was a powerful one, directed against Indians. He had ranched and farmed at a time when Indians and whites hated each other bitterly, and sniped at each other constantly. He could never understand why we put Indians on reservations—he would have preferred to see 'em armed and on the warpath again, so the question of who owned the West could be settled in fair combat. It pained him to see his fiery old adversaries penned up and going to waste.

Uncle Billy bought a Dodge sedan in 1925, a beautiful black job, and he became an excellent driver in his seventies. I think his feeling about Indians was the only indication of his wanting to bring back the old times. With the better part of a century of hard and often bitter labor be-

hind him, he was never one of those men who complain sourly about how modern generations are going to the devil, and getting lazy, and have no more spirit of free enterprise, and so on. He knows there was a lot of romance in the old days and he loves to reminisce, but when he found that an automobile would get him where he wanted to go faster and more comfortably than his horse, he sold the horse and bought a car. He was overjoyed when electricity became available to La Luz, and when I last saw him, in his middle nineties, he thought the telephone and the radio the hottest things ever invented.

He looks formidable, with his bristling white mustache, his fierce, bright eyes, his own teeth still in his mouth, and his wiry little frame. But he was always tolerant of people, and except for an occasional outburst of amazement at one of Pop's more spectacular "projects" I never heard from him a real criticism of his son or his grandsons. He believed each man should make his own life, in his own way.

During the first years in Mountain Park my mother was a little steadier than Pop, but not steady enough to be a manager. She had flights of fancy herself, and indulged them. However, her fancies did not involve packing up a family, abandoning a farm, and drifting off to faraway places, and she never hesitated to remind her husband of this fact when he criticized her.

Both my parents were a little hazy about money values. Pop was one of those guys who's never broke, but always just a little in debt, and never able to scrape much capital together at any one time. He'd been banged around rather badly overseas, but he was scrupulously honest about his pension: he was offered a one hundred per cent disability because the gassing had given him very bad chronic asthma, yet he would take only ten per cent, or ten dollars per month, because he felt he could work ninety per cent of the time. He belonged to the American Legion for a short time, and quit huffily when, as he said, he discovered it was nothing but a chiselers' club trying to strip the taxpayers.

Once a veteran showed up at Mountain Park and built himself a handsome and rather expensive house in a valley above us. He and Pop hit it off well until Pop found that the fellow, who seemed in fine health, was getting a tremendous pension—enough to loaf for the rest of his life—because he'd been in some noncombat job, had had some operation on his innards, had alleged it was due to war injuries, and had cashed in. Pop would never speak to the man again.

Although Pop's restless ways caused my mother to lead a rather hard life at times, I remember being impressed at a very early age with his devotion to her. She was inclined to be indulgent with Sid and me, and she paid the inevitable price: while we knew we could put things over on her, we took her more or less for granted and weren't as considerate in many ways as we might have been. Pop constantly reminded us of our duties to her, without too much success.

She and Pop tried hard to conceal their routine quarrels from Sid and me, but kids know about those things. Pop was a blusterer; mother was the wounded doe type. Her eyes would get large and stricken, she would become very quiet, and yet under it all she had an immense stubbornness. Her favorite technique was to start a long walk, generally in the direction of Alamogordo, when she was mad at Pop. She'd strike off down the road, knowing she presented a pitiful and lonely little figure. Pop would glare after her for a while, then we could tell his imagination was going to work: A tourist, roaring drunkenly down from Cloudcroft, was going to flatten her with his automobile, or maybe she was going to fall down a mountainside and break her leg. Pop would jump into whatever vehicle was handy at the moment and go retrieve her, as she always knew he would. Occasionally he would delay a little too long (once she almost got to La Luz); then she would have forgotten her original mad and have become furious all over again because he'd let her walk so far.

I remember that trick of hers was a regular source of embarrassment to Sid and me. Other parents slugged it out with monkey wrenches and kerosene lamps in the privacy of their homes; people always knew when my folks had been at it, because they'd see our mother walking sadly down the pike.

My grandmother Bemis's little place was bounded on the eastern, or uphill, side by the Mountain Park Baptist Church, a pretty, white frame structure set in a shady plot of ground covered with cedar trees, under which were benches and tables for summer picnics and sociables. The church had rows of hard folding chairs, with benches in the rear to accommodate the extra worshipers who came when there was any special service which promised excitement. My parents were reasonably pious people; they taught Sid and me to say our prayers regularly, but they never forced us to go to church. They didn't need to; when Sundays came along, there was seldom anything else to do, and most of the kids in the community "worshiped" regularly.

For a long time my mother, who could play a piano accurately and with some style, was the Sunday organist. The church had one of those wonderful old foot-operated pump-organs, guaranteed to work up a sweat on the hardiest player. The church was never locked, and because of its proximity to our place my mother used to enjoy going up occasionally during the week and practicing. Sometimes I went along on practice days, got down under the stool, and worked the pedals with my hands while she whanged out the "Battle Hymn of the Republic."

Sid and I used to play in the church sometimes when nobody was around. We discovered that when a bass note was held down and the pedals were pumped up vigorously and then allowed to collapse slowly, the organ sounded exactly like an airplane droning overhead and fading away into the distance. By holding down several bass notes, a whole covey of bombers could be made to go over.

Because the community was not big enough to support a regular preacher for long, most of our ministers were transients, either working a circuit or just passing through and in need of practice. We got some corkers that way. I guess they all came under the general heading of Baptist, but that covers a lot of ground. We got more than our share of hell-and-brimstone boys and evangelists.

All the evangelists spent the regular eleven a.m.-to-twelve preaching time working us up for a night service, promising all sorts of excitement and revelations, and they

generally had an overflow crowd for the evening. The church was lit with Coleman gasoline lanterns, which were very bright and glary and attracted all the moths in the countryside. Each preacher usually had a wife who played the organ, so my mother was done out of the honor at most of the evening services. Anyway, her music was the light kind which brought visions of blue skies and harps, and most of the evangelists wanted gloomy stuff which spoke of doom.

With the organ giving out the proper background music, the preacher would work himself into a frenzy and beg us all to come up and be saved. There were two or three regular sinners who could always be depended upon to start bellowing and sobbing and carrying on Sunday after Sunday, but sometimes nobody else broke down and the burden fell on the youngsters of the community. Partly because of the excitement and thrill—and partly, I think, because we didn't want any preacher going to another congregation and saying we were a bunch of pikers —we kids, who usually sat on the benches in the back, would start nudging and whispering to each other:

"You go first . . ." "Nah, you wouldn't follow me— you go first . . ." "Go on, hurry up . . ." And one of us would get to his feet with a red face and a self-conscious grin, and start faltering up the aisle toward the preacher, who stood there with sweat and a dedicated look gleaming on his face. Several more nervous little sinners would come stumbling along behind the first one. Halfway up the aisle we always regretted having left our seats.

"AHHH!" The preacher always screamed, "Here comes a child of Christ, to be received in His forgiving arms! Come on up, sonny, don't be scared. Don't be afraid of the Lamb of God!"

I was never sure whether the preacher meant himself by

"Lamb of God," but he certainly never looked like any lamb. As he welcomed us at the top of his voice, scrapings and rustlings could be heard as the adults craned at the little souls about to be saved; even the organist paused and turned to look.

We'd all line up and pass the preacher one by one; he'd mumble "God bless you" at us and pat us on the head and shake our hands in a man-to-man way, and we'd go back to our seats, saved and proud. It got to be a regular racket, for, as I've said, we changed preachers often. All the younger set got saved on an average of twice a month. Sometimes a preacher would come back for a return engagement, and note something familiar about the looks of his new converts to Christ, but generally enough time had elapsed since the last appearance so that he couldn't be sure.

However, we kids got trapped once. An especially energetic evangelist informed us one Sunday morning that he had pressing business elsewhere, and so would have his big doings in the early afternoon instead of that night. The festivities started right after lunch, and all the kids delivered handsomely, some ten or twelve being saved. This time we didn't get away. The preacher said such a glorious saving must be clinched by a real baptism, before our newly cleansed souls could slip back into error.

So every car and truck in the churchyard was pressed into service and the entire congregation roared down the mountain to Tularosa, a town on the plains twelve miles north of Alamogordo, where there was a church with a real setup for baptism. The preacher rattled along triumphantly in his car behind the procession, possibly to make sure none of the kids made a quick leap for safety.

The Tularosa church had a reservoir, almost big enough for a swimming pool, under the pulpit's platform, exposed for use by simply lifting a section of the floor. As soon as we were all safely inside, the preacher, fully clothed, leaped into the pool up to his waist and began taking us on, one by one, and ducking us completely under. I caught a bad cold from riding back to Mountain Park in the back of somebody's pickup truck with my clothes plastered to me, and I never went back to be saved again.

It was in our little Baptist church that I discovered I had a flair for demagoguery. I'd go up there alone sometimes, stand behind the pulpit, and deliver political speeches. My parents were Republicans, for some strange reason, and my political leanings and knowledge at the age of seven were about equivalent to those of Little Orphan Annie. It was the year Hoover was elected—I was very pro-Hoover. Also, I knew several of the old sayings about thrift and hard work.

"Vote for Hoover!" I would yell. "A stitch in time saves nine. A penny saved is a penny earned."

But I ran out of political material in a very short time, and took a fling at preaching. I waved my arms and exhorted the imaginary congregation to turn to Jesus. I found my sermons were much more effective when spiced with profanity. A line from one of my favorite spiels went like this:

"Come up, come up, you dirty old sinners from hell, and bury your heads in Jesus' lap. Look at those innocent little bluejays flying around in the piñon trees outside, and nest-ing in the cedars! You, too, can have wings and nest in the cedars if you turn to our Saviour. Come up, you damn old sinners, and be saved!" This kind of talk put me right down there with the sinners, I felt; made me one of them, so to speak, and it was better to approach them from that angle than to stand up there and scare them with a holier-than-thou attitude.

The Mountain Park-High Rolls grade school, a rather handsome fieldstone building with several classrooms, large windows, pleasant toilets, and a good-sized auditorium, sits on a flat place on the side of a hill which overlooks the lower end of our farm. When I started attending, there were several dozen students of all shapes and sizes. The school had an immense old iron bell hung in a loft high over its front porch, with a rope hanging down to swing it. It was quite an honor for a kid to be allowed to ring the bell, for it could be heard all over the countryside.

There was a kind of merit system attached to bell-ringing; you had to get excellent grades or something. I remember I was doing well in one class for a while; it was presided over by an intense young teacher named Ward Curtis—he was the postmaster's son—and he let me do the bell-ringing often. But one day I made a pest of myself— I kept running up to him and asking if it was time for the bell, until the poor man became so exasperated he told me I couldn't ring it again until I learned some patience. Whereupon he went out to ring it himself. One of the pivots which supported the bell had crystallized and the whole works, weighing well over a hundred pounds, came crashing down on his shoulder, shattering a number of bones in his upper torso and putting him in the hospital for months. I always felt it was my fault, somehow.

The school playground was a small affair, large enough for basketball or softball, but not both at once. It had no slides or swings or other paraphernalia of a grade school— only a battered basketball, a softball, and three bats. One day my Pop, in a mood for a minor project, rattled up to the schoolyard with his truck full of two-by-fours, scraps of lumber, and a drive shaft from an extinct Reo, with the universal joint still attached at one end. He'd decided the school needed a carousel.

Pop set the rear end of the shaft into concrete for a solid base, then constructed a ten-sided, cone-shaped merry-go-round, big enough to carry twenty kids, two on each section of the platform, with handholds so they wouldn't tumble. The wonderful thing about the contraption was that it would not only go round and round, but it would bob up and down, for he'd hung it from the universal joint at the top of the shaft. We all had a howling good time with it; our favorite trick was to entice a lot of suckers onto it, preferably girls, and get it spinning crazily enough to upset the sturdiest little stomach; we kept them going until they were green and had to excuse themselves from class periodically for the rest of the day. Unfortunately, the school was small, we'd exhausted the suckers in a very short time, and the carousel fell into disuse.

The auditorium had an excellent stage, and every year the kids had some sort of play. Toward the middle of my

second or third grade, someone decided on a "Tom Thumb Wedding," one of those horrors primary schools used to love to put on, and I found myself cast in the hero's role, as Tom Thumb himself, the handsome groom. This pleased me mightily. I made the first three or four rehearsals, then caught a series of head colds. A mere cold means nothing to a true Thespian, especially if he has the top role and his leading lady is the local forest ranger's daughter, a lissome thing of five, who's stirred the first tender feelings of love in his heart.

But my mother was a worrisome person; she made me stay home when my snuffling became loud and wet, which caused me to miss many rehearsals. The hero's role was passed to someone more dependable. I was crushed and sulky, through with acting, and I hoped the roof of the auditorium would fall in the middle of the play.

But Tom Thumb's wedding wasn't through with me. Through some quirk of nature or some ingredient in the food which all prospective fathers in the vicinity had eaten a few years before, practically all my contemporaries had been born male, the forest ranger's daughter being one of the few exceptions. The play needed bridesmaids desperately.

I howled in protest, but the very parents who had rooked me out of the hero's role now betrayed me again.

"He'd make a cute girl," my mother said, and she swung my father around to this point of view. It's a wonder it didn't scar my id or my libido, or whatever it is, for life. Of course my brother Sid was enthusiastic; we'd reached the age of intense rivalry and he saw in this an opportunity to make me suffer forever. In El Paso I had a female cousin several years older than I; my folks wrote her folks and sure enough, she'd outgrown a "most adorable" party dress with a long skirt, one which could be hooped. The awful thing arrived; my mother hooped it and fitted it to my squirming form. The night of the play I was smeared with make-up, my short hair was covered by a flowered hat, and I was sent backstage to meet the lucky male who was to be my companion onstage. I had no lines to speak, no acting to do; I was to just stand around and make like a charming bridesmaid.

My escort turned out to be a surly character three years older than I. He was in my grade. I didn't like him because I thought him stupid; he disliked me because he didn't like to be in the same grade with someone he considered "young enough to be his son," as he once put it. The oaf saw me come in all prettied up, and glory be, he didn't recognize me! His eyes lit up (I *was* rather pretty) and he fell for me like a ton of bricks. When I started to step over some object backstage, he sprang to my side and gallantly held my arm so I wouldn't stumble. It was disgusting, but

I had sense enough to keep my mouth shut and smile prettily at him from time to time, for I knew there would be hell to pay if he found out who I was.

The first part of the play went off all right, all things considered. I don't remember much of it, except that I'd actually begun to hope I'd be able to get home in anonymity, throw the female duds in the stove, and enjoy, for the first time in my life, the job of scrubbing my face.

But somebody, perhaps my brother, spread the word. I knew it was all up with me when, during intermission, while the adults who had supported this dramatic monstrosity were outside smoking and chuckling, my escort pushed his way through several other actors and came at me with the most withering glare of contempt and revulsion imaginable.

"Sonabitch," he said. He placed a rough hand on my trembling, maidenly bosom and shoved me on my dainty can with a loud thud. He turned his back on me and on the play and walked out of the building, and we didn't see him again for several days.

Afterwards everybody commented on what a fine bridesmaid I'd been; the adult males with some ribaldry, the ladies with genuine admiration, and the kids with unholy leers.

My favorite teacher was a lady named Frances Godley; she found that I liked books, and she felt kindly toward me, for she liked books too. This mutual admiration society we formed led, of course, to several characters charging that I was teacher's pet. Although some time had passed since the Tom Thumb Wedding, I felt my stock was not too high among my fellows, and set out to erase the accusation. I remember concocting a note to one of the young local belles, in large block letters, inviting her in the most loathsome language to come to my house and sleep with me. I posted this note, under the awed stares of sev-

eral boys, on a conspicuous fencepost along the road home, where I knew the girl would pass and it would be called to her attention. My compadres were open-mouthed, for they knew what the results would be.

The fact that my age and experience made the note one of history's most futile amorous invitations seemed to be no defense when Mrs. Godley confronted me with the note in class next morning. The girl had, of course, found it and given it to her.

Perhaps it was the language in the note that made it objectionable, I don't know. Anyway, Mrs. Godley went out to a clump of willow shoots, cut one of adequate size, and wore it out on me, in front of the class. I bore up well under the sting, for while it was painful, I felt it was clearing me of the unjust stigma of being teacher's pet. My relations with Mrs. Godley continued good after that; I think perhaps she understood what my motive had been.

Sid and I had started in the same grade together; we both came to hate school, for entirely different reasons. Sid was a very active character physically, and like Pop he loved to tinker around with mechanical things. School was a big waste of time so far as he was concerned; this attitude was shared by most of his friends, and he got along well with our contemporaries.

I liked the school itself, but didn't care much for some of the people in it. Sometime in my infancy I'd developed a case of rickets, with the result that my head was somewhat oversized for the rest of my frame, or rather, my head was normal, but my body was too small. It wasn't much of an affliction and it didn't keep me from helling around, but it did let me in for a certain amount of ragging. I got very sensitive about my head (and my ears, which stuck out atrociously), and would occasionally tangle with someone who passed a remark about my looks, usually a kid out of my weight class and with disastrous results to my person.

I became a very roosterish little character, known as an

easy mark for a teasing. Often a perfectly well-meaning young buck would kid me or shove me in a friendly, cocky, boisterous way; I would flare up, regarding it as a studied insult, and would reply with such fury that I would find myself possessed of another enemy. I didn't make many friends.

The fact that I didn't mind schoolwork and liked to read didn't help matters at all. Robust kids don't like book-worms, unless the bookworm goes far out of his way to get along with them, which I neglected to do. After a verbal or physical tangle, I'd go home, get a book or a magazine (I didn't lean toward the classics at all—I preferred trash, and the bloodier the better), read a while, then dream of going off somewhere, getting rich and powerful, and coming back to take revenge on the thugs who didn't appreciate me.

So Sid and I, at the age of nine and eight, each for his own reasons, were happy when Pop got that gleam in his eye we'd come to know quite well even at that age, and began talking of conquering new worlds. My poor mother was just beginning to relax, the farm being in good shape at last and some comfort in sight; she listened fearfully while Pop talked about how Mountain Park held no future for people like us.

Sid thought of new country to see and new things to tinker with; I thought of getting the hell away from that school and the still-fresh memories of such fiascoes as the Tom Thumb Wedding and my six latest fights, and starting afresh with new kids, preferably some with heads and ears just like mine.

"Take Arizona," Pop said. "That's new, fresh country." So we got ready to take Arizona.

Although my brother later turned out to be an expert trader, Pop's deals always seemed to work to his disadvantage. Either he was too softhearted or too susceptible to flattery. Thus, although he'd started with a brand-new Model T, the truck for which he traded it was very flimsy, and the old Maxwell touring car which replaced the truck, for our Arizona adventure, was an even sorrier machine. But the junk pile behind the house, which contained the most amazing assortment of old metal and machine parts, produced enough material to put the Maxwell in running shape.

We bundled into it with our baggage, several extra tires of assorted sizes, and Blackie, a tiny dog the color of anthracite coal which Pop had bought for a dollar from a street vendor in Parral, on the assurance that he was a pure-blooded "Boston Terrier." The fiery little beast had endeared himself to me by biting off the end of my brother's nose, and to the rest of the family by being an aggressive and noisy watchdog who was determined to let neither the moon nor the Cloudcroft train come near our place.

We roared out of Mountain Park and down the steep road toward the plains with no fanfare; a man standing near the post office shrugged his shoulders hopelessly as we passed him, as if to say "There go the Mauldins again," and his little boy watched us with what I was sure at the time was envy.

Part Two

ALTHOUGH WE LOOKED LIKE RESPECTABLE
tourists and not like Steinbeck characters, we did start the
venture with very little capital, which ran out as we
reached the eastern outskirts of Phoenix, Arizona. We had
not started without a plan—Pop intended to take one of the
homesteads in the desert west of Phoenix, which were then
being offered freely to veterans, and to develop it into a
citrus farm, for he'd heard that country was rapidly growing into a great agricultural area, the climate being such
that two crops a year could be brought in.

Alone, he'd probably have gone on out to the homestead
and started from scratch, cash or no cash, but he had a
wife, two sons, and a little black dog to feed, so he stopped
at the edge of Phoenix, set us up in a camp in a sheep pasture, after making a rental arrangement with the owner,
and went into town to look for work which would keep
us supplied with necessities and would build up a little

capital for the desert "project." He got a job changing tires on Greyhound busses. It was heavy work, but it paid fairly well. Sid and I had a fine time in the sheep pasture. There were plenty of shade trees, it was grassy and cool, and we slept in hammocks. Our tent was stretched between the Maxwell and a tree. It was a very pastoral scene.

Unfortunately, the depression came along, and just as it had begun to look as if we were going to be able to start the homestead with plenty of funds, the Greyhound job collapsed. Soon we were almost as broke as we'd been when we first arrived. My folks made a heroic effort to put by as much money as possible, but Sid and I ate a lot, wore out our clothes very quickly in the sheep pasture, and we all loved going to a restaurant in town and then seeing a movie occasionally. We couldn't go to the homestead just yet.

We were beginning to get a lot of neighbors in the sheep

pasture as the depression got worse and worse. Finally Pop, in desperation, took a job picking cotton. I think it was the only "career" that ever really hurt his pride. But while he was very improvident in many ways, he refused to let his family be underfed or badly clothed, and if protecting them meant cotton-picking, he was going to pick the damn stuff. He never let us forget we were proud people—not foolishly proud, but we weren't bums and he wasn't going to let us look or feel as if we were.

Once, when we were all feeling pretty low during the cotton-picking job, Pop came home to the tent all sore and defiant, with blisters all over his hand.

"Get dressed up," he said to us very grimly. He took us into Phoenix, where we ate a magnificent meal in a good restaurant, and saw not one, but two movies—one at the Orpheum, the most expensive place in town. It took several days' pay, but it was Pop's way of spitting in Fate's eye. He never railed at Sid and me for loafing around the sheep pasture and having fun all day while he sweated on the job. He'd have died rather than have his kids out picking cotton. I think it would probably have been very good for us, but that's how he felt.

Things looked up when we got a lead on a job at Romola, a citrus-farming development near Litchfield, some fifteen or twenty miles west of Phoenix, and we moved there. At that time the country around Litchfield was becoming what is now one of the most prosperous citrus areas in the West; it was the same sort of thing Pop was ambitious to do with our own homestead (on a smaller scale, of course). Monster pumps were used at Romola to bring up water for irrigating the thousands of desert acres, and Pop took a job caring for the pumps. He figured to kill two birds at once: he expected to learn many of the tricks of desert agriculture, and to make enough cash so we'd have a good start on our own place.

In the Romola settlement we had a small house and were able to have some sort of family life. It was decided that Sid and I should get on with our formal education, and we were enrolled in the Litchfield grade school. The town itself was several miles away; my mother, looking around for something to occupy part of her time and augment the family income, had the happy idea of running a sort of school bus to haul all the kids from the settlement to town.

Every morning and evening, the old Maxwell touring car roared across the desert, sounding like a fighter plane in a power dive (its muffler had fallen off somewhere between Mountain Park and Phoenix), leaving a tremendous plume of dust behind, packed to the gunwales with squirming, fighting, laughing, snuffling kids. All the regular students at school looked in wonderment and awe at the pack of dusty desert rats that arrived for studies every day. Sid and I were very proud of our dashing mother-chauffeur.

A lady teacher at Litchfield was the first of a long line of teachers I had, right up through high school, who felt it was a sin and a shame that I should be left-handed. To some teachers it must have seemed like a deformity. I was stubborn about it, and I worked out an answer to the Litchfield pedant which was so successful that I often used it on later teachers. She was one of those devout souls who's always talking about God: "If God intended this, or that, He'd have done it that way." So I told her that if God had wanted me to be right-handed, He'd have fixed it.

She knew I was being uppity, but I had said it in such an innocent manner that she was stuck. She kept a sharp eye on me. I had other troubles with her. We clashed over the pronunciation of "pigmy": she wanted it pronounced "pij-my"; and of "often": she insisted that we sound the "t."

When the "pij-my" trouble came up, she made me stay during a recess, brought a dictionary to my desk, and stood over me triumphantly, probably intending to make me pronounce it or write it a thousand times when Webster proved me wrong, while I looked it up. When I showed her the pronunciation, she was so angry and frustrated she took it out on a friend of mine, a Mexican boy, and my opinion of her went to an all-time low. When he came to class after recess, she made several remarks about Spanish-Indian ancestry, directed at the room at large, but since he was the only Mexican boy, it was obvious who she was after. It seems she was offended because he needed a haircut. After commenting on his slovenliness for a few minutes and embarrassing him horribly, she directed him to go up to her desk so she could inspect his head for lice. The

Pigmy
Often

unhappy boy let out a wail, leaped out of his seat, and ran out of the school. He never came back.

Southwestern customs in regard to minorities could be very confusing to a small boy. There was no segregation between Mexicans and Caucasians in schools or theaters, therefore the kids mixed and played together, yet social mingling was frowned upon, and there was a definite feeling of tension between the two groups. The Mexican boy who ran afoul of this stupid teacher was popular on the playgrounds, and he and I had become quite pally in class, because he sat across the aisle from me and liked to draw pictures as much as I did. We'd often exchange them. Yet the class, while it was excited by this episode, which broke up the dull day, felt little resentment toward the teacher because of the scene. Had the boy happened to be a Caucasian, his parents would have been roaring at the doors of the school within an hour, and there would have been an awful scandal.

The delicate distinctions between playground friendships and social mingling had been demonstrated to Sid and me at Mountain Park before we went to Arizona, when we both became very chummy with a Mexican boy who was a star student at the school. His report cards showed nothing but "A's," yet he was likable and popular in spite of it. He was a very handsome kid, with the looks of a Spanish aristocrat. Sid and I invited him to have supper and spend the night at our house once; he hemmed and hawed and said he'd see about it. He was wiser than we. For when we told our parents we'd invited him, they were faced with the difficult task of explaining the facts of life to us. It didn't make sense to me then, and it still doesn't, but that's how it was.

After school and during weekends, Sid and I would wander all over the huge Litchfield development, watching buildings and machinery go up. Sid loved the machines; he knew what made them all tick, and he was a favorite with the men who ran them. There were carpenter shops where they'd let us fool around making little wooden things on the lathes, and metal shops where we'd salvage old scraps and rods, take them home and play with them.

Most of the large permanent buildings around the development, such as mess halls for the workmen, were being constructed with adobe, the cheapest, sturdiest, and most practical material in that dry climate. I struck up a friendship with the chief adobe mixer. He showed me what kind of dirt to use, how to mix in straw and other binders to hold the huge mud bricks together, and how it's poured into a mold and left to bake in the sun. I remember once he told me why the mess hall for which he was making bricks at the moment was going to be an especially good job—the adobe would last forever, he said, because it contained the finest ingredient you could get: ground-up workman.

"Every time a man gets caught in the machinery at one of the pumps and is all mashed up," he said, "they pound up the carcass in little bits and give it to me for my adobe mix."

He said most workmen were careful, and of course they couldn't kill a man in cold blood for the purpose, so not every building was lucky enough to have the ingredient.

"That's why some of the buildings," he pointed out, "start cracking and sagging pretty soon after they're finished."

He said this current batch was going to be especially fine because it had three men in it. I sat and watched, fascinated, as he stirred the stuff; I looked for rings, watch chains, bits of clothing, or recognizable fragments such as fingernails.

"It's mostly the blood that does it," he said, reminding me, for proof, how fast blood clots and hardens when a finger has been cut. He said even one mashed man improved a building a lot, even though a large structure stretched a single body pretty far. I believed him implicitly, and always hoped my Pop would be careful around the machinery and not end up as an adhesive factor in his own monument.

The huge development was rapidly turning a large portion of Arizona desert into an oasis; looking around at it kept reminding Pop of his original aim to make our own modest little oasis. Finding that in spite of ourselves we'd saved a little money and could get on with the project, Pop filed for 320 acres (a "half section" in realty parlance) in the desert sixty miles west of Phoenix, near what has since become a tiny spot on the road map called Tonopah. With his usual talent for being worsted in such deals, he swapped the Maxwell for a decrepit Chevrolet truck. (We were always going from car to truck and back to car again.) We loaded our belongings and rattled out to our new home.

It was smack in the middle of nowhere, twenty-two miles by a very dusty corduroy road from Hassayampa, the nearest village. Our 320 acres was populated by greasewood brush, four hardy rabbits, a Gila monster (which we subsequently captured), seven thousand-odd rattlesnakes (including sidewinders), half a dozen Palo Verde trees, and an ancient ironwood tree, which, we were later told by a man who claimed knowledge of such things, had been there since way back in the B.C.'s. A cluster of low hills bounded the place on the west, and the flat land was gashed by several small eroded gullies and washes.

It was late in the spring of 1930; the sun slashed down like an acetylene torch; heat waves and mirages danced gaily all around so that you could never be sure of the exact position of the ranges of far-off mountains or of the ancient, volcanic peaks which studded the desert floor. It's an awesome sight when a peak or a whole range of mountains waltzes gaily some thirty degrees to the left or right while you watch. A lonely peak five miles southwest of our place had the frivolous habit of duplicating itself on certain days; often it would give birth to twin baby peaks which would stand for hours, shivering gently, before disappearing

The air was burned dry and clear by the sun; the only limits of vision were the curve of the earth and the irregularities and dancing habits of the terrain. Hills forty miles away seemed to be within easy walking distance.

There's an old joke which could have originated at any of the great flat countries of the West where the air is clear and distances are deceptive, but which has been claimed by the desert people in Arizona as well as by the ranchers of the Northwest plains. Seems a tourist, camping on the desert for the night on his way to California, rose early and decided to stroll to a nearby mountain and back before breakfast. He returned late in the evening, footsore and half dead of thirst, never having got near the mountain. Weeks later, he was walking with a friend across a California field. They came to a tiny irrigation ditch; the friend stepped across, walked a little way, noticed the tourist was no longer with him, and turned in time to see the tourist undressing and preparing to dive into the stream and swim across.

We were mountain people, and at first glance this desolate inferno was pretty appalling; but within an hour we began to discover that the desert in Arizona has many beauties. For one thing, the heat didn't make us miserable, even though its intensity gave you the feeling of a fresh-baked muffin. The air was so dry that it soaked up perspiration immediately, serving a double purpose—it gave you an aura of evaporating moisture (or steam) for insulation, and your clothes didn't become wet and sticky. Your lungs felt very fine and pure; you knew no germ could live an instant in that air. Once your eyes got used to the glare, there were all sorts of fascinating colors and planes and perspectives all around the horizon. And greasewood gives off a pleasant perfume, dry and tart. But in spite of all this it took a lot of imagination to think of our place as a potential oasis.

We pitched our tent in the middle of the property, set up very light housekeeping, then bumped about the desert to take a look at our neighbors. A number of people had homesteads in the area, the nearest being some four miles from our place. Most of them were families like us, who'd come to the desert for hopeful economic reasons. A few were afflicted with ailments, mostly lung trouble, and had come simply to make homes and try to keep living. One or two were well-off financially, and building their houses for them turned out to be a small source of income to the heads of other families, most of whom were farmers and so were reasonably skilled in carpentry.

One of the first families we met, and one with which we became very good friends, were named Robinson. They'd discovered an immense stream of hot mineral water under their property, and were planning to make their place into a spa where people could come to flush and sweat ailments out of their innards by drinking and bathing in the water. I think it was the Robinsons who gave Pop the unhappy facts about water in the desert—wells cost $2.50 a foot to drill, casing was expensive, and more often than not a driller had to go more than two hundred feet down for water, if he hit it at all. And pumps cost a lot. We just didn't have that kind of money.

We found that even drinking and washing water had to

be hauled a considerable distance in barrels, from a place called Winter's Well, which had a windmill and storage tank. The price was 45 cents a barrel, which held fifty gallons, so it was almost a cent a gallon. That was all right with

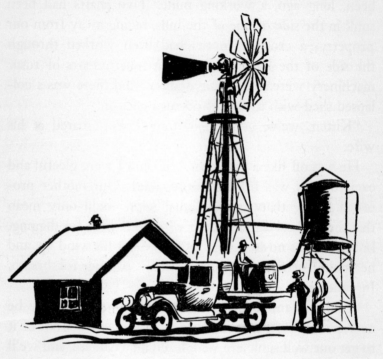

Sid and myself; we had the usual kid-prejudice against washing and saw a chance to escape frequent ablutions on the excuse of economy. But it threw an awful damper on Pop's oasis plan because even a small orange tree would drink several hundred dollars' worth of water, at those prices, before bearing its first fruit.

The Robinsons would have given us barrels of mineral water free for drinking purposes, but we couldn't expect them to irrigate an orchard for us. We felt pretty downcast at first. However, Pop brightened very quickly when he explored the hills bounding the western end of our little homestead and discovered the remains of what had been, long ago, a working mine. Two shafts had been sunk in the side of one of the hills, facing away from our property; a crosscut tunnel had been worked through the side of the hill into the deeper shaft. Parts of rusty machinery were still scattered about, and there was a collapsed shed with a roof of corrugated iron.

"Kitten, we've got a gold mine!" Pop roared at his wife.

He was off like a ball of fire. Sid and I were gleeful and excited: this was real glamorous stuff. Our mother protested feebly that an abandoned mine could only mean that the original diggers had run out of reasons for digging, but there was no stopping Pop. He'd got his wind up, and he spoke for fifteen minutes, hardly pausing for breath. In conclusion, he said:

"I don't want to get rich on this mine. We'd only be corrupt if we got rich. I figure we'll pull enough out of it to get our well sunk and we'll build a nice house, and we'll have the best citrus farm in Arizona."

There was some talk about what kind of shade trees we'd use to line the driveway to our house and whether we'd have a stable and keep saddle horses for pleasure. Sid and I agreed that even after we closed the mine to avoid the corruption of riches, we'd sneak out and pick up a nugget from time to time for a spree at the Orpheum in Phoenix.

Pop had already acquired a buddy, a young, redheaded bachelor named Pat who'd started a homestead five or six miles away. Pat had a temperament not unlike Pop's; it took him no time to get infected with gold fever and agree to become Pop's partner. They were pretty sure the mine was on our property, but just in case any future boundary trouble should arise, the two of them filed a claim in traditional style—by putting it in a tobacco tin and burying it under a cairn of rocks at the crest of the hill which contained the old workings.

Pop and Pat were ready to begin plundering their treasure immediately, but my mother, who showed a remarkable lack of enthusiasm for the mine—considering it was going to make our fortune—insisted that first we have something to live in besides the tent. She had a prejudice against rattlers climbing over our feet and tarantulas and centipedes getting in our ears while we slept at night.

Reluctantly, Pop engineered a house, a simple, one-room affair which took a very short time to build and was perfect for that climate. It had a wooden floor, raised six inches off the ground. (This became a favorite rendezvous for diamond-back rattlesnakes passing through on their way to work and wanting shade for a ten-minute rest, and I guess they were grateful, for they gave us no trouble. Occasionally one would rattle a lazy greeting to a new arrival—this made my mother very nervous at first and she'd go after them with Pop's old Army .45, but she got used to it after a while.)

The walls of the house were three feet high; a framework was built up another three feet and covered with

wire screen, which gave a view all around the compass
and allowed breezes to come through. Canvas blinds were
hung outside, above the screens, so they could be rolled

down for privacy: although privacy from what, we were
never sure. Arched roof supports, made of bent planks,
were covered with half our tent, which we cut up for the
purpose; the other half was tacked to the underside of
the beams for a ceiling. The inch of air space between the
two tarpaulins made fine insulation against the sun.

A screen door was set in one end of the house and a
double bed at the other. Above the double bed Pop con-

structed twin bunks, laid end to end, for Sid and me. The beds were curtained like Pullman berths and were quite private. Scraps from the floor and wall lumber made serviceable chairs and benches. It was a very comfortable layout.

During the house's construction several neighbors dropped around from time to time to help, for in that country a lot of the old pioneer spirit still persisted. So many of them commented on the ingenuity of the tent-house that Pop actually got enthusiastic about it, despite his impatience to get at the mine. Before he was through he'd built a fancy outdoor kitchen on the shady side of the house. It had a counter equipped with stools, a stove and cupboard, and a gay awning. It was like an open-air diner, and it became so popular with friends that if they hadn't helped with the construction we might have printed menus and installed a cash register.

The materials for the house had cleaned out our capital, and the minute Pop had completed an outdoor privy and enclosed it with a framework (covered with El Toro cement bags he'd picked up somewhere) and my mother admitted that everything was reasonably comfortable, he and Pat set out for the mine, to make their first million, with Sid and me trailing behind.

Nobody could tell the age of the gold mine. The remains of bulky machinery and the traces of tool sheds showed someone had invested capital in it—probably a branch of one of the big mining corporations. Several individual prospectors must have come along and worked it later; bits of clothing and camping equipment, including a rusted-out coffeepot, were scattered about.

Pop and Pat explored the two old shafts in the side of the hill, near the top. One was very deep. It bent to one side about thirty feet down, and we couldn't see the bottom. Sid and I dropped rocks into it, then waited for what seemed like minutes before the rocks, rattling and bounding and sending up spooky echoes, hit bottom. One medium-sized rock struck the ancient wooden ladder which went down the length of the shaft, and shattered a rung. Obviously it was much too rotten to support anyone. Just above the bend a platform had been built around the ladder; beside it was the dark mouth of a horizontal crosscut tunnel which came out some distance down the slope.

"If there hadn't been the most ore in the deep shaft they wouldn't have dug so much there," decided Pop.

"Yeh," said Pat.

"We ought to test the air down there before we start fooling around."

"Yeh."

"Know anybody with a canary? We can let him down in his cage and if he comes up sick or dead the air's no good."

"The Delaneys have got a canary, but you try borrowing him to let down in this hole and you'll get shot. Try letting a candle down and see if it goes out."

So they lit a candle and let it down gently on a cord, while Sid and I hung over the edge and watched. As they tried to maneuver it past the platform which made a landing at the intersection of the crosscut tunnel, a draft from the crosscut caught the flame and blew it out. They went downhill to the crosscut's mouth, walked through the tunnel, and started lowering the candle from the landing, while Sid and I remained above, watching them and listening to their voices come up hollowly.

"Hey, Pat."

"Yeh."

"The damn thing caught on the ladder in the bend. It won't go down any further and I can't get it up."

"We ain't ever going to find out how the air is down there."

"Pat."

"Yeh."

"Listen, why didn't we think of this before? This shaft is older than the other one. Why would they start the other one if they hadn't dug so deep in this one they'd huh used up all the ore?"

(My mother had thought of this first.)

"B'God, that's right."

"You know, we'd have to build a new ladder if we used this shaft, and a hoist to haul up the ore."

"Yeh."

So, having conveniently reversed their logic, they abandoned the deep hole and concentrated on the smaller one, which had a fairly good ladder, and on the crosscut tunnel, which was shored safely enough with heavy, only slightly decayed timbers.

They took ore samples from both, crushed them into powder with a heavy old iron mortar and pestle some former miner had abandoned, and panned the ore, using drinking water from our canvas water bag hung on the door of the truck. Pop was very adept at the panning operation. Sid and I watched, fascinated, as the water gently swished the rock particles from the tunnel back and forth in the pan (they used a washbasin they'd borrowed from our house).

A little was spilled out each time, until finally a fraction of a teaspoon of matter remained in the bottom. Pop and Pat were joyful at what they saw, but I remember I was disappointed. Out of the great quantity of rock with which they'd started, I expected to see at least a cupful of brilliant yellow treasure. Pop had me look at the tiny bunch of rock particles very closely, and among them I saw a few very sparse flecks of dull metal which they told me was gold, possibly a nickel's worth. I couldn't see why they were so happy about that.

The sample from the shallow shaft seemed richer than that from the tunnel—it contained maybe six cents' worth of gold. They started poking about in it, taking more samples and panning them, while I went to investigate

the crosscut. Sid and I had been around Pop long enough
to know better than to behave foolishly around deep holes
and other places where kids often get hurt, and I knew
a long, dark, spooky tunnel like that might be a popular
clubhouse for the local rattlesnakes, so I went in with two
lighted candles, one in each hand.

Because it sloped slightly upward from the hillside en-
trance to the opening in the deep shaft, a cool little breeze

blew through the crosscut from time to time. When I was
about halfway through, the breeze came in a gust and
blew my lights out. A rattle came at the same instant. It
couldn't have been worse-timed. The tunnel echoed it and
I couldn't place it. Clutching the candles very tightly, I
began a fearful retreat, stepping backwards. I thought of
dropping the candles and picking up one of the bits of
timber scattered about the floor, for a weapon, but in that
dark I wasn't enthusiastic about grabbing up a stick which

might begin wiggling in my hands. The thought of it chilled me, and suddenly the whole place seemed full of rattlers.

A rattle sounded again; this time it seemed behind me and directly under my feet. I reversed my direction with a jump—and the rattle came from ahead. A person can stand just so much. I shuddered, took a deep breath, and sprinted back the way I'd come, comforting myself by thinking the rattle at that end had sounded punier. It would have taken a fast snake to get me as I shot out of the tunnel, hung a foot on a rusty piece of corrugated metal roofing, and went sprawling down the slope on my belly, in a spray of old ore and pebbles.

I sat up, an old man. I still clutched the two candles. The piece of tin which had thrown me was shaking and clanking from the impact. It rattled and buzzed loudly. Then a breeze came up the slope and rattled it more gently, sending its vibrations into the tunnel, with a dry, reptilian sound. As I marveled at this, I realized that I had a whole box of safety matches in my pocket and that it would have been simple to relight my candles in the tunnel. I never went back in there.

Pop and Pat scratched around their shaft all day, loading the truck with samples. Next day they took them to an assayer in Phoenix to have the gold content analyzed. They came back somewhat discouraged—they'd been told they had gold all right, but that they would make more money hiring out as ditch diggers than working that mine. It would take tons of such ore to produce enough gold for a medium-size wedding band.

But after they'd sat around the house and talked awhile —Pat, having no family, spent his evenings with us—they perked up and got infected with gold fever all over again.

"Hey, Sid."

"Hunh?" Pat was the only man I ever saw who could get such short replies out of Pop.

"You know treasure hunters."

"Uh-huh."

"You know, Sid, sometimes they dig for weeks without getting anything and go away, and then some fella comes along with a shovel and takes one scoop and finds the treasure."

"By God, you're right."

They decided that whoever had worked that mine before had stopped just a fraction short of exposing a great vein of pure gold. After all, the little sprinklings of it had to come from somewhere, didn't they? The source must be just one more shovelful down.

The two hopefuls went back to town and returned with several cases of dynamite, little round tins of detonator caps, and great rolls of fuse, guaranteed to burn at the rate of one foot per minute. Pop had worked with explosives before, mostly in the Parral mine, and once he had frightened the life out of Mountain Park residents, during the period when he was making our place over for a tourist heaven. At the lower end of the farm is a beautiful field, marred by a very unsightly bog about fifty by a hundred feet. Several cows and horses had, in past years, grazed on the lush vegetation which grew on the crust of the bog, and had broken through and disappeared. Nobody had any idea how deep the thing was, and no amount of prodding with long poles had located the animals' bodies. Pop had decided to blow off the crust with a high explosive, dredge out some of the muck so that the bog would have clear water on top, then fence it in, stock it with fish, and have a nice pond. Accordingly, he filled a twenty-foot length of iron pipe with almost a whole case of dynamite, put a long fuse into one end, making what was possibly the world's greatest firecracker, and shoved the entire length of the pipe into the bog. It was a spectacular explosion. The ground jarred, windows rattled for miles around, geysers rose from holes in the bog's crust and splattered the field with muck, the crust itself heaved, billowed, buckled, and settled back, quivering indignantly. Nothing was accomplished, but it had been terribly exciting. Pop loved dynamite.

He was very happy blasting around in his own mine. He and Pat would drill deep holes in the rock and shale on the side of the slope with a ground-auger. Pop would gently tamp a number of sticks of dynamite into the hole with a piece of hoe handle. He generally used a lot of explosive, but Sid or I, or both, would always sit nearby and urge him to use more. He would slit the last stick and insert one of the detonating caps, into which he had crimped a length of fuse. He did the crimping with his teeth—a colorful old practice barred in regular mines, because the fulminate cap is a deadly and sensitive little thing which has blown the jaws off many crimpers. This last stick would go into the hole with the others, Pop would plug the hole with bits of rock, fray the end of the fuse, light it, and walk leisurely away, trusting the foot-a-minute guarantee of the fusemaker.

He or Pat would clamber to the top of a high rock, cup hands about mouth, and bellow "FIIIIIIRE!!!" There never was anybody around for miles, but the traditional warning yell was very dramatic as it rolled down the slope, echoing against rocks, and fetched up against a far hill. Pop and Pat always did things properly.

We'd all get behind rocks and the charge would go off with a satisfying *CRUMP*, hurling debris high in the air in a thick cloud of blue-brown smoke. We'd be back at the hole before the last pebble had fallen, and Pop and Pat would furiously shovel out the shattered rock, while Sid and I hung over them, hoping to see a great vein laid bare.

They'd been working and blasting one especially promising-looking spot for a number of days until it was six or eight feet deep, when Pat decided he had become a demolition expert from watching Pop, and announced he would set off the next charge. When the hole for the charge had been bored, Pat disappeared into the workings with half a dozen sticks of dynamite, a cap, and three feet of fuse. I remember Sid wasn't there that day: he was helping around the house. Pop and I sat fifty yards or so to one side of the hole, listening to Pat fuss around and watching the heat waves and mirages dance in the great expanse of desert we could see from the hilltop. I was anxious for Pat to finish because they were going to let me give the "FIIIRE!!!" yell for the first time, and I was very proud.

There came a sudden, terrible, jarring thud. We spun

around toward the hole in time to see Pat's khaki shorts
—all he'd been wearing, except for his shoes and hat—rise

high into the air, lazily turning over and over, atop a
geyser of dust, rocks, and dirty smoke. Horrified, and
oblivious of the bits of rock which whizzed down all

around us, we watched the drawers flirt about as they reached the apex of their climb, stop almost still as the smoke dissipated, then come tumbling down in tatters.

Pop and I stared at each other. I didn't want to go back to that hole and see what was left of a man who'd had the pants blown right off him, and neither did Pop, who'd actually seen explosion victims before and didn't have to use his imagination. But we had to do it. I started crying, and I suspect Pop wasn't far from it himself. We had thought a lot of Pat, with his flashy wit and his wide, freckle-faced grin. With me snuffling and Pop whistling through his nose, we went over to pick up our friend, re-assemble him as best we could, and take him to Phoenix where he could be glued together and buried.

At the edge of the hole I remember I had to use every ounce of my will power to look in. Possibly I mightn't have succeeded had not a sudden "Good God Almighty" from Pop startled me into looking. There was nothing in the hole, just a jumble of freshly broken rock and a thick haze of blue, acrid powder smoke, the smell of which I'd always enjoyed before. It was more awful, in a way, to find Pat atomized than it would have been to see his mangled body.

We were staring into the hole, looking for something, anything, to take to Phoenix for burial, when Pat, all of him, stepped out from behind a clump of rocks—where, after lighting the fuse, he'd hidden while we'd been watching the desert—and started guffawing at us. He looked sort of funny himself, clad only at his extremities, in hat and shoes. He'd laid his shorts on top of the charge before sneaking out of the hole.

"Ye' damn near killed us!" Pop roared. I've never seen him so furious. "Y' goddam fool, some of those big rocks almost came down on the sprout here!" And in truth, several had. We'd been much too near the explosion for safety. Livid, Pop leaned over and picked up a rock the size of his fist, and I think he would have heaved it at Pat and sent him flying across the desert if the fellow had been better dressed. There's something ludicrous and helpless looking about a man standing there in front of you like that, naked as a jaybird.

I started laughing at Pat and then Pop broke out in chuckles and Pat started guffawing all over again.

But we had the last laugh. When the practical joker retrieved his shorts and started to put them back on, he found the blast had rent them fore and aft, in the most strategic places, so that he looked nakeder with them on than off. He had nothing else handy to cover himself, not even a handkerchief, and he was to eat with us that evening.

"Hey, Sid," he said, "you know that grease rag in the truck? It's awful dirty but I can wear it until we get to your place and I can borrow a pair of your britches."

"Go to hell," said Pop.

"Sid, I can't go to your house like this. I gotta wear something."

"Nothing doing. I'm gonna burn that grease rag right now, and if you try to stop me I'll bust you wide open with a rock." Whereupon Pop got the rag out of the truck and touched it off with a match. It burned very quickly on the ground, and every time poor Pat, who was holding his torn drawers with one hand, made a move as if to save the rag, Pop lifted a rock threateningly.

Pat went home to supper with us, having fixed his shorts sideways, like a breechclout, and tied them in position with strings. Some other friends had also come for supper; Pop refused to lend Pat a pair of his own pants, and he tipped off everybody, so that my mother wouldn't let Pat have even a towel. Pat was a shy man; he spent a miserable evening with the ladies staring at him and the men ribbing him.

Dynamite is expensive stuff; when Pop and Pat were down to their last case they despaired of finding the "big vein" right away, and decided to see how much value could be extracted from the surface ore which had been dug by former miners, and to save the last case of dynamite in case they should get a fresh lead on the vein while poking around the surface. Assays had showed the debris on top of the ground had about as much gold as the shafts and the crosscut tunnel. Pop and Pat made a deal with a Phoenix mining concern, which obligingly parked a railroad ore car on a siding near Hassayampa, twenty-two miles away, and they undertook the task of filling the huge car.

It was backbreaking work. They'd shovel and grunt and strain until they'd loaded the protesting little Chevvy truck, then haul the load to Hassayampa, heave the stuff up over the high sides of the ore car, then come back for

more. After many days of this the car was filled and hauled away. Within a week they got a check which looked immense—but when the amount was broken down it showed that they had worked twelve to fifteen hours a day, blistering their skins and ruining their backs, for three dollars per diem apiece.

They were thoroughly disgusted with the mine. They could have made much more money at almost any other enterprise. Only Sid and I were content about the project, for hadn't our father had a gold mine? How many kids could say the same?

Fifteen years later, while driving through Arizona, I stopped for a look at the homestead. The house had long ago been broken up and carried away, presumably for firewood. The only trace of it that remained was a small heap of useless auto parts—what was left of Pop's old junk pile behind the house. At the mine I found two men with a little camp and a 1928 Chevrolet they'd converted into a pickup truck. It was half full of ore. The men were resting in the noon sun, and I asked them how much they made out of the mine.

"It comes out about three dollars a day apiece," they told me.

About the time Pop and Pat decided to give up the mine the Fourth of July rolled around. Near Winter's Well a little grocery store and post office had recently been set up, and somebody conceived the idea of having a big community party there on the Fourth. Most of the families had enough money in the sock to buy a few firecrackers for the kids, but it was decided that if everybody would pool their money, we could all have a magnificent fireworks display—much better than popping puny and individual firecrackers around the desert.

Sid and I had been celebrating the Fourth for weeks in advance—we had not overlooked the fact that Pop and

Pat had bought many more dynamite caps than they had needed for the mine. The vicious little brass detonators, about half the thickness of a pencil and two inches long, came packed fifty to the round tin box, with a warning on the label to keep them away from heat or jarring influences. They were much more deadly, in proportion to their size, than the dynamite they were designed to tickle into exploding, and they were far more spectacular to set off than any giant firecracker.

Sid and I swiped whole boxes of caps from the mine, took them far out in the desert—where nobody would hear them and get worked into a foolish frenzy about our safety—and experimented with them, using six-inch lengths of fuse, which gave us thirty seconds to get away after lighting them. We made dandy hand grenades by pouring a handful of pebbles into the hole in the top of an evaporated-milk can, then inserting a cap with fuse attached, pushing the soft tin lip of the hole tightly around the fuse for a seal, lighting the fuse, and chucking the affair into a greasewood bush, where a lizard or two could usually be found taking a siesta. If there was a lizard in the bush, we got him, for the pebbles and fragments of tin laid down a deadly little shrapnel barrage.

We found that regular bombs could be made by filling a can completely with pebbles, then inserting three or four loose caps beside the one with the fuse. The fused one would set off the others with eminently satisfactory results.

The caps made our stovewood foraging expeditions easier. Any large piece of wood, even the amazingly tough desert ironwood, would split nicely when coaxed by a dynamite cap inserted in a crack at one end. Sid and I carried on our own little mining expeditions with the caps, blowing holes in the ground and in the sides of gullies and then poking around for nuggets. All we ever brought up was an occasional shell-shocked tarantula.

We'd expended all our caps when time came for the community fireworks, so naturally we went along for the fun. The party started just after dark. Sid keynoted the affair by trying to handle two Roman candles at once, with the result that a fiery ball from one of them shot into a small pile of skyrockets, setting off one which roared into Sid's pants leg, ripping a hole in it and scorching his calf. This inspired other youngsters into similar feats of bravery. Two older boys had a contest to see who was the braver: they stuck a bit of glowing punk into the ground, and each lit a firecracker from it simultaneously, the contest being to see which one would throw his cracker last.

It was a great show. The kids lit up the sky while the grownups made merry inside the store, each homesteader sampling and mixing the others' special types of home-made refreshment, with results as pyrotechnic as anything the tots were doing. Harried wives scuttled from sons outside to husbands inside and back again, cautioning all to take it easy.

Rather early in the festivities, when I had been cavorting about in the desert with a sparkler in each hand, making weird designs against the night, I galloped in to get a fresh supply of sparklers, and noticed Pop and Pat, walking not too unsteadily, go out to our truck, get in, and drive away. That's funny, I thought: Pop and Pat love parties. They must be sore at somebody. Wonder how we're going to get home? I grabbed a handful of sparklers, lit two, stuck the rest in my back pocket, and danced out into the night again, making figure eights. I was starting to do the alphabet in Spencerian scrolls when it struck me all of a sudden what Pop and Pat were up to.

That last case of dynamite, the one they'd saved from the mine, had been in the back of the truck when we drove to the party. In fact, I had sat on it. Sticking my burning sparklers into the ground so I could come back to them later, I started running toward the store, two hundred yards away, so I could be the first to tell everybody the exciting news that Pop and Pat are gonna give us all a big surprise, I betcha.

I had covered perhaps a fifth of the distance when a mighty blow clapped me on the back and I was on my face in the dirt, with gravel and fragments of greasewood whistling over my head. Several of the more sturdy boys in front of the store managed to keep their feet, although they were stung by flying debris. The building suffered somewhat, and a window went out, but nobody was cut by glass.

When I reached the store, everybody was standing about in clusters and murmuring in awed tones. The kids had forgotten their fireworks. What possible thrill is there in a mere Roman candle when the whole desert has suddenly exploded? Like magic, Pop and Pat, looking very scratched and disheveled and sober, appeared in the midst of the crowd, saw that a confession would lead to a lynching, and made themselves inconspicuous by babbling like everyone else.

"What happened? What happened?" they kept saying. "We were standing there talking and something knocked us off our feet. My God, what was it?"

Nobody could answer them, but everybody had his suspicions, for who but Pop and Pat had been banging away with dynamite at a mine during past weeks? The culprits, who had realized too late that they'd put much too short a fuse on much too much high explosive, wisely kept their mouths shut, and so did I. Next day an inquiry about the blast came from a place three miles our side of Hassayampa, or nineteen miles away.

Sid and I had turned a deep chocolate brown within a week after we'd started living on the homestead. No adult dared go out under the powerful sun without a hat, and why Sid and I failed to get sunstroke is a mystery. We wore nothing but shorts or denim pants, and those were for decency, not protection.

Our part of the desert had long ago been volcanic country. The very top layer of ground tended to be gravelly and littered with large and small fragments of formerly molten rock. Some of these were an intense and beautiful black, so smooth they would take a brilliant

polish; others were red or blue or crystal clear; and some rocks, looking twisted and boiled and tortured, contained every color of the rainbow. The temperature went as high as 130° on summer days, and any exposed rock became hot enough to fry an egg. Sid and I actually did fry one for fun—it took about fifteen minutes before all the white hardened. We didn't eat it.

Despite the intense heat of the gravelly ground, we took to chasing around barefoot. A few days were enough to develop very hard calluses. Traveling was a technique: we would hop and skip across an open stretch, like Hindu fakirs going across beds of coal, and make for the nearest bush in line with our destination. The instant our feet hit the comparative coolness of its sparse shade, there would be an intense, sharp pang as the heat generated on the outer layers of callus penetrated through the inner layers and knifed into the nerves in the soles of our feet, but the pang would go as quickly as it had come and the wonderful coolness would soothe us.

As soon as our feet cooled we would race across the open space for the next bush. Since the greasewood was scattered thinly and we could seldom find a series of bushes in a straight line along our route, this technique made for zigzag traveling. It was much more fun than wearing shoes. Shod, a walk across the desert was just a walk; barefoot, every journey was a challenge and an adventure. We had to pick our erratic course carefully before starting, spotting bushes as far as we could see, then lining up more when we had reached the last of these. And it was very important to pick alternate routes, in case a bush two hundred yards distant should change its position or disappear entirely as we approached it, as a result of the tricky heat waves.

We learned a lot about traveling from the lizards; they used the same technique. They were cute little fellows, very friendly and curious and harmless. When one of them would undertake a huge trip to a bush fifty yards away, and his tiny feet got unbearably hot on the way, he would flop over on his scaly back, wave his feet in the air to cool them, then flop back over and scurry on. We couldn't imitate this particular stunt, for our backs had no protection at all. The only desert creatures that didn't seem to mind the midday heat were the horned toads, little monsters from one to three inches long, with saucer-shaped bodies, sharp tails, necks ringed with collars of vicious little spikes, and faces so horrible they would scare you to death if they weren't so small. Actually, the creatures were fairly congenial, and if we kept our fingers out of the way of their prickly horns, we could hold them in our hands and stroke them on the back: they'd arch their backs in joy, then flatten out and fawn at us. We believed implicitly that if you picked up a "hornytoad" and failed to caress him, he would spit in your eye and blind you.

One of the most incongruous of all the desert creatures was the terrapin, or desert turtle. These grew from four inches to more than two feet in diameter. What they were

doing in that country is a mystery to me. With chassis designed for water, they are ungainly and pitiful waddling around among the hot rocks. But the turtles seem to make a good living at it, and they are well protected from all perils, carrying their own combination parasol-and-armor.

Outside of the fact that we had to carry snakebite kits (a tiny aspirin tin, containing a single-edged razor blade for gashing, and a few grains of potassium permanganate

—our belts were for tourniquets) and know how to use them, the desert was a wonderful place to play, and Sid and I had a lot of it all to ourselves.

We never fretted much about the diamondback variety of rattlesnake: they are big, easygoing fellows who always gave us a warning rattle when we approached. A human being represents a waste of venom to them, since he can't be swallowed and there is no other use for him. So long as man keeps out of their way they want no part of him. But their small, gray brothers, vicious devils called sidewinders, are not so accommodating. They have plenty of poison and they have rattles, but nature wasted the latter on them, and should forthwith reclaim them and give them to some more deserving viper. Sidewinders love to nail people unawares.

Hating the sun, rattlers curl up under rocks or bushes during the heat of the day. Considering the huge snake population of western Arizona, it's surprising that Sid and I had only one really bad time with them. One bright, hot day the two of us were out bush-hopping and headed for a very large greasewood whose shade promised to give balm to all four of our feet at once. Sid got there first, and he stepped right on a sidewinder who'd been snoozing in a flat coil. It was all the snake's fault. It had no business out so far from the roots of the bush, where snakes usually stay.

The calluses on Sid's bare feet were pretty thick—he didn't realize what he was standing on until the sidewinder awakened, squirmed, decided the weight on its back was unbearable, and determined to rid itself of the burden in the only lethal way it knew. It drew back its nasty little head and let fly, but because it hadn't been coiled for a fast strike, and Sid had become jet-propelled

some two or three millionths of a second earlier, it missed. Like a spooked horse, my brother took the bit in his teeth and ran wild through the desert, screaming,

"Kill it, Billy, kill it!"

"Kill it yourself!" I screamed back. "I'm not goin' near

it!" From the instant I'd seen him step on the sidewinder I'd remained rooted where I was, three or four yards from the bush, although my soles were beginning to smoke.

After a while Sid wore himself out and came panting back to kill the snake, which by this time was fully coiled in battle position and darting its head about, looking for blood. The little bum still hadn't rattled. Sid smashed the sidewinder with a dead greasewood stick (which he inspected very carefully before picking it up), then we both started for home, avoiding all shady bushes on the way. Our feet were in pretty bad shape when we arrived.

All the days we'd been running around among the bushes we'd known there were bound to be snakes in them now and then, but after a while we hadn't really thought about it, because usually we hadn't seen them, all camouflaged among the rocks, wood, and spotty shade. For two weeks after the sidewinder finally did scare the life out of us, we wore shoes, losing our calluses, and when at last we got over our fright, we had to go through the painful process of toughening our soles all over again.

Rattlers around our place had two nonvenomous cousins who were their deadly enemies—king snakes and bull snakes. Both kings and bulls loved to chase rattlers and tangle with them. So far as I know, the rattlers always lost these battles and were eaten, but I've never known how they were beaten. The kings and bulls were constrictors, so evidently they were able to crush the rattlers while avoiding their fangs. Once I was startled by the sight of a huge diamondback wriggling frantically over the desert rocks at midday, and I wondered what on earth had him so excited he'd scorch his tender bottom like that. Then I saw a slim, wicked-looking king snake whipping along in pursuit about twenty feet behind, and gaining every second. He was only half the size of his quarry. The rattler saw a small gopher or jack-rabbit hole and hurled himself into it so hastily that a cascade of pebbles and dirt tumbled after him. The king snake shot into the hole with amazing speed and a sort of deadly grace.

I ran to the hole and put my ear as near to it as was consistent with safety, should either the rattler or the dismayed legal tenant come hurtling back out. I would have given anything to have been able to watch the scene below —the horrified rodent housewife cowering in a corner of her parlor and trying to shield her wailing children from the flashing bodies of the two terrible gangsters who'd battered down the door, crashed in, and were now locked in lethal combat. At least that was how I imagined it. I waited nearly an hour, hearing nothing, and nobody came out. Probably the king snake ate the rattler and had Mrs. Rodent and children for dessert, in which case he was so swollen he couldn't get back through the hole.

Another time, near a place belonging to a family named Olsen, I came upon two bull snakes, of rather small stature as bull snakes go, all tangled with each other as if they were fighting. I hadn't known bull snakes were cannibalistic, and was very curious. I watched them for a while, then walked over to the Olsens' house (they had a thirteen-year-old son with whom Sid and I sometimes played) and asked them what they thought of what I'd seen, describing the snakes very carefully.

Mrs. Olsen's face assumed a strained expression, Mr. Olsen looked embarrassed, and the son, who was a worldly character, guffawed loudly and said, "Don't worry about it, Billy, they were *prob'ly* married." I went away entirely dissatisfied and confused.

The rattlesnake's most feared enemy was the roadrunner, a most unbelievable bird unless you've seen him. He's a comical-looking mixture of ostrich and mongoose, with somewhat the appearance of the former (in miniature, of course—he's not much bigger than a pullet) and the temperament of the latter. He probably got his name from autoists in the Southwest, because his greatest joy is to hide beside a road when a car approaches, then run across in front of it, causing drivers who have never heard of him to pass a hand over their eyes and proceed at a cautious ten miles per hour to the nearest oculist.

The roadrunner has long legs and a thin neck. Two or three scraggly feathers perch foolishly on his tail. He has a terrible beak, long and sharp, and he wears a single bright feather sticking cockily straight up from the top of his head. His silly little wings aren't worth mentioning. Possibly he uses them as ailerons to bank his curves, for he runs at great speed.

His mongoose blood comes out when he finds a rattlesnake. Just like Kipling's Rikki-tikki-tavi with a cobra, he dances about the deadly snake, teasing him into striking. A roadrunner is one of the few creatures on earth that can move faster than a striking snake. When a rattler attacks and misses, he is helpless for a second—having extended himself almost his full length—until he can gather himself back into a coil and strike again. It is at that help-less instant that the roadrunner pounces from the side and gives the snake the works, right behind the head, with his wicked beak. Then he eats the snake.

I never saw a roadrunner nail a rattler, but I know two people who have seen it and described it to me. So far as I know, the roadrunner depends on venomous snakes for food, which explains why the funny little birds are revered in the desert.

One of the nastiest and most poisonous desert creatures is the scorpion. A big one can kill a small boy, and Sid and I were often warned accordingly. One day we found a monstrous scorpion near our tent-house—his body was fully four inches long, with his striking tail curled over his back. My mother bravely tackled him with a rake and he gave her a good battle while Sid and I cheered from the sidelines. She would make a pass at him with the rake, and he would scuttle out of the way. Each time the steel tines came near him he'd strike them. He was so big and tough we could hear the "ping" when he hit the metal. He must have had a very sore tail by the time she finally impaled him.

Sid, who had almost been had by the sidewinder, got himself stung on the hand by a scorpion once. It was a little one, so all Sid suffered was a swollen hand and a very sore arm. He seemed to get all the breaks. The only close shave I could brag about was my imaginary rattler in the mine tunnel.

In a way, it's wrong to call that part of Arizona a desert, for "desert" brings to mind Saharalike expanses of barren sand, endless and flat. Not only was our country broken up by hills, small mountain ranges, and occasional green spots where the water level came near the surface and where clumps of trees and grasses grew, but the colors of the landscape were often breath-taking.

The sunsets would make sentimentalists out of brass monkeys. In fact, I would recommend them to brass monkeys, for those sunsets are really very tiresome after a

while, sort of like a Cecil B. DeMille technicolor production or a feed-store calendar. They seem contrived. Many artists have been attracted to that desert, and it's interesting to note that the hacks always go to work on the sunset, splashing every bit of their color on their palettes and smearing it on the canvas. They murmur reverent platitudes about how "Only God could paint that picture. No mortal can capture it; we can only make poor copies." Disgusting. And it's the same with the photographers. The hacks use filters and fancy films and come up with blazes of glory which are forthwith printed on postcards and sent home by tourists with no imagination.

The good artists and photographers turn to the desert's real colors: the subtle hues of the land itself, as the sun changes hills and valleys into rose and gray from deep blue in the early morning, then golden gray, then a variety of hot colors until noon, when everything becomes glaring white and black, then deep red at sunset, lavender and purple at dusk, then the desert turns back to deep blue with silver highlights under the moon, or simply gray-blue under the stars. Desert colors are mysterious blends of many things, and that's why good artists consider them a challenge, and ignore the sunset, which any child could copy by throwing buckets of paint at a wall.

Winters out there are wonderful, for the days are steadily balmy, with never a chill, and the nights are just cool enough to make one happy, but never cold enough to require a second helping of blankets. Because of the dry air, during all seasons you can watch rain clouds pile up thirty or forty miles away, start dropping their load of water in a slanting gray mist, then see the rain become absorbed and fade away long before it hits the ground.

Occasionally, however, the rain clouds get their heads together, grumble a bit, and gang up on the desert. The first assault wave, made up of shock-troop clouds, sacrifices itself to dampen the atmosphere, then before the air can digest it, the reserves come through and turn the dry land into a soggy mess.

Our first desert flood came about three months after we'd settled on our homestead. I remember going to sleep one night listening to the sound, which we'd almost forgotten in that dry climate, of big raindrops hitting the roof. Our canvas top made a pleasant drumming sound which put me to sleep very quickly. Next morning it was pouring so hard I felt as if the falling water would beat me to my knees when I stepped outside. Just for a stunt—we really didn't care for baths—Sid and I took soap outside and had a fast shower and shampoo.

Near our house a shallow, sandy-bottomed wash, about two feet deep and fifty feet wide, had become a terrifying river which roared and boiled past, slopping over its banks and whipping bits of wood and brush along so fast we could hardly follow them with our eyes. Fascinated, I went over to it and stuck in a tentative toe; a crest came along, caught my foot, and almost yanked me in. It was what's called a flash-flood. Several foolish tourists are killed every year by flash-floods in the Southwest. When they see the weather pile up threateningly they camp in sheltered-looking gullies. The water doesn't wet their feet and climb gradually, awakening them and warning them in the middle of the night—it comes in a solid wall, bowling over and smashing everything in its way, even automobiles sometimes.

It happened that we were short of groceries that morning, and we decided to drive to the store and stock up, in case the rain should continue and the roads wash out. The four of us piled into the tiny cab of the truck and set out, with Pop having to drive with his head in the rain because even if the windshield wipers had worked, which they didn't, they couldn't have kept the glass clear. It was as if a fire hose were playing on us.

The store was on a little rise straddled by two shallow washes like the one near our house. For some reason they carried only a six-inch deep stream at the moment and we splashed through easily. Four or five other families were at the store, everybody jabbering about the big rain and speculating on how long it would last. The kids all scrambled around playing in the downpour and inventing games like throwing sticks into the fast-moving water and trying to hit them with rocks before they were whisked away. After a while we all hit on the idea of making a raft, and started looking about for planks. The grownups kept gabbling away, and what with one thing and another, by the time somebody thought of looking again at the washes, they were regular rivers. The rain showed no signs of letting up. The whole lot of us were marooned, for both washes joined a mile above and two miles below the store.

Nobody was really unhappy about it; we kids were overjoyed and even the parents considered it something of an adventure. What better place could one ask for a marooning than a grocery store? The day passed very pleasantly. We finished our raft, a big one, but since we knew better than to try to launch it until the stream quieted down, we turned to roughhousing and other games, never once going inside except to eat. We were probably the cleanest-washed kids in the world that day.

A few bottles always appeared mysteriously when four or five of our fathers got together, and the storekeeper had a gallon jug of high-quality amber. The ladies did as all ladies do; they gabbled and murmured and cut the throats of the ladies not present on our little island.

Then the terrible cigarette famine struck. The man who came in a panel truck once a month from Phoenix and supplied the store with cigarettes, pipe tobacco, roll-your-own, and chaw, had been due that very day but had obviously been washed out somewhere on the road, and

the store was out of stock. The men took this very calmly at first. They rationed out the few cigarettes left in one man's pack and left the store's one remaining sack of Bull Durham on the counter, with a pencil and paper beside it and each man's name inscribed across the top. Every time anyone made himself a cigarette he was on his honor to make a tally mark under his name, so everything would be equal. When the "Bull" was gone, a butt hunt developed. Unhappily, most butts had been thrown out the door, in consideration for the host's floor. The rain hadn't let up a bit, and only a few pitiful and soggy butts were still intact on the ground. The paper on most of them had been dissolved already and the tobacco washed away.

The poor devils retrieved the few intact butts, lovingly dismantled them, and spread the wet tobacco on a table inside, brushing every crumb of it into a paper bag as soon as it had dried. Rolling cigarettes from the crumbs, then rolling new ones from the ends of these, kept things going for a few hours. The smokers used needles from the store's "sewing department" to pierce the butts and hold them when they burned too short for the fingers.

Finally, an expedition was made to the cars and trucks to search for forgotten butts or whole cigarettes which might have dropped to the floorboards or been left in compartments—each man ransacking another man's vehicle. The tobacco situation had seemed funny at first, but it was getting serious, and by this time nobody could be trusted to share anything he might find in his own property. There was a brief celebration when the storekeeper (I can't remember his name) found three whole cigarettes, real tailor-mades, in a pickup truck, behind the seat.

Nobody thought to look under our truck's seat. All the time I knew an almost-full sack of Duke's Mixture was there, because that's where I kept it, the truck cab, when it was parked near the house, being an excellent place for me to sneak for a smoke. Duke's Mixture cost a nickel.

I wasn't sure when I would get my hands on another nickel, so I kept my mouth shut during the cigarette hunt.

But when the unhappy fellows began rolling cigarettes of coffee from the store's supply, coughing and gasping and driving the ladies to distraction with clouds of acrid smoke, I started feeling ashamed of myself.

I began to remember how Pop, even when he was picking cotton at Phoenix, had never begrudged Sid or me a movie or a toy car or an ice-cream sandwich; and how, on the Christmas of the year Lindbergh flew the Atlantic, Pop had worked a solid week carving me a perfect scale model of the "Spirit of Saint Louis," and had paid a quarter for a magazine just so he could cut Lindbergh's picture out of it and paste it into the window on the side of the plane. It had been a broke year, and on Christmas night Sid and I had overheard Pop telling our mother, almost with a choke in his voice, how badly he felt because he didn't stick to one job and make enough dough to buy us good presents. As if the plane hadn't been a good present.

Thoroughly disgusted with myself, I took the Duke's out of its hiding place and took it inside to Pop, who was noisily strangling on a coffee cigarette. Every man in the place pounced on me and whooped happily. One of them even whisperingly offered me a drink of good corn whisky.

"I was playing in the back of the truck and look what I found under a piece of canvas," I told Pop, looking him more or less straight in the eye.

"Thanks, son," Pop said graciously, knowing damned well whose Duke's it was, because neither he nor Pat smoked the brand, and he had become pretty sure that I was addicted to the weed.

A sack of Duke's will make some forty-odd smokes, rolled thin, and the forty butts will make ten or fifteen more, producing, altogether, about fifty or sixty from a full sack. My sack made about forty. It was enough to get the sufferers through the night and part way through the next day.

We spent the night in the store and in the owner's house. There was some singing and a great deal more talk during the night, with the kids going to sleep sprawled around the floor on blankets and quilts. The rain droned on and the washes rumbled. I remember waking up several times during the night, looking drowsily at the men sitting around the stove (it wasn't lit, but there's something psychologically good about sitting around a stove) and smoking my Duke's, being careful to inhale every drag and not waste a puff of smoke. I felt the great peace of one whose conscience is clear.

Late the next day the washes had dropped and slowed enough to allow us all to plow through in our assorted vehicles. We never did have a chance to use the raft. On the way home, the desert looked like a Midwest valley after a dam has broken. There were thousands of lakes of all sizes. And yet, as soon as the rain had stopped completely, they were sucked into the earth even more quickly than they had been formed. Within a day they were nothing but messy puddles of mud. After the second day they were almost dry, and on the third day the mud had hardened and cracked into desolate, ugly, jigsaw patterns.

After the rain we found tiny casualties everywhere—tarantulas and kangaroo mice and bugs that had been drowned and washed up out of their holes. We hoped to find a large portion of the rattlesnake population drowned too, but evidently the heavens look out for the bums. We didn't find a single rattler, and not even a scorpion. Only an old bull snake, who looked more like a case of hardened arteries than a drowning. Sid and I cut off his head and skinned him, peeling him inside-out like taking off a sock. We cleaned the skin, turned it right-side-out again, and nailed it to the house to dry, intending to make a belt or something out of it, but we never got around to it.

We noticed that our wash had changed considerably as a result of its flood. The bottom was gouged in spots, it was littered with debris, and its sandy bottom was streaked with peculiar black powder which Pop recognized as iron the rain had washed from an ore bed somewhere along the line. He had a little magnet among his collection of tools and junk (already our yard was piled high with the inevitable "spare parts" pile), and Sid and I spent hours dragging the magnet along on a string in the bed of the wash, stopping every minute or two to strip off the clusters of pure iron particles and put them into fruit jars and tin cans. We collected pounds of the stuff and were thinking of going into business when Pop reluctantly parted with the information (he'd been happy to see us engaged in such a harmless undertaking instead of trying to blow ourselves up or get snakebitten) that a thousand boys with a thousand magnets would have to work weeks before enough iron was collected to make it worth while hauling it to town. We promptly gave up the whole operation.

Misguided city dwellers often move to remote and sparsely populated areas with the idea that they can have secluded and private "retreats," where neighbors mind their own business. Actually, the more thinly settled a country is the less this is true. Little quirks in people which pass unnoticed in busy cities become glaring eccentricities in the country, and a man is known for his eccentricities rather than his accomplishments or failures.

There was a homesteader on our desert who made friends with lizards. A bachelor, about sixty years old, with a small income or pension, he had built himself a shanty and planned to live out the rest of his days happily and peacefully under the sun. He was an interesting and likable man, and a very friendly one, but kids stayed away from his place because he talked to his lizards. There were several dozen around his shanty—he gave them flies, named each one and called it by its name. He always knew when a nest of new little lizard eggs had hatched, because, he claimed, mamma lizards always brought the babies around to show to him.

I don't know whether the perky little reptiles could really be tamed and taught tricks, but we had heard that this fellow had not only taught his lizards to do such things as balancing on their tails, but that he could speak lizard-language. We believed it. We credited all sorts of tales about him, and new ones came up every day. To us there was something hideous and frightening about a man who consorted with lizards.

Yet this was the same kind of character who feeds pigeons in New York's Central Park, who coos at them on the steps of the Art Institute in Chicago, and who chatters at squirrels on the Boston Common, exciting no comment other than an occasional "Isn't he sweet? I bet he's awful nice to his kids."

And the Olsens (to whom I'd gone with my questions about the two bull snakes I'd seen "eating" each other) were Seventh-Day Adventists. Had they lived in a city, nobody would have noticed what day they went to church, or even whether they went to church at all. But they were the only Adventists on the desert and it made them terribly conspicuous. Their son, with whom I went on snake-killing expeditions and other stimulating sorties, had a special air about him, so far as I was concerned, because of his father's religion. I used to drive him nuts with questions about Adventism.

Once word came out to the desert that an eastern Jew had filed for a homestead. I overheard a little cluster of men in the store discussing ways and means to keep the fellow out of the country, or to run him out once he had arrived. Either the rumor was false or the man changed his mind, for he never showed up.

My folks made friends with a homesteader who had a special glamour—a Swiss who'd been in the Russian revolution. He had a pretty wife who was an artist and who tried, without much success, to teach me how to color my own drawings. The Swiss fascinated me because I loved war stories. I had driven my father to distraction pestering him for tales of France, and now I had a fresh source of material.

The Swiss had been, he told me, a "white," and the other side was "red." Or rather, he'd been a white sympathizer; the Russians he was living with at the time of the revolution were some sort of aristocrats. I was a little royalist at heart. One of the great disappointments of my young life had been getting the information, from a reliable source some months earlier, that the king of England no longer wore a crown and an ermine robe to breakfast, and no longer boiled his enemies in oil. The fact that right in our tent-house sat a man who'd been a guest

of some prince or count really titillated me. I was nuts
about the pageantry of royalty; somebody in my family
still has a snapshot taken of me, at the age of six, in the

back yard of our Mountain Park house, sitting in a large
armchair covered with a fancy blanket like a throne, wearing a fur collar of my mother's, a crown I'd made from

yellow paper, and holding an egg beater for a scepter. I had spread our only good carpet on the dirt and grass and had wrestled the big chair onto the center of it, then laid the hall rug from the back door to the main carpet, so I wouldn't soil my feet on the way to and from my throne. I sat in that chair for hours, condemning to hideous tortures people who'd teased me at school.

I made the Swiss tell over and over again the best part of his story: how the reds had slaughtered the entire family before his eyes. I could visualize a horde of savage fellows with vermilion skins butchering men, women, and children, who had pale, chalky faces. I made him repeat the part about the reds putting him up against a wall before a firing squad. In the first telling, he refused the blindfold. I remember marveling that the crimson beasts had the courtesy even to offer him a blindfold. In the next telling, he threw the blindfold into the face of the officer commanding the firing squad, and at the third telling he spat on the officer's shiny boots. The story never got tiresome because it improved each time. Of course, the Swiss would not have subsequently been there in our tent-house talking about it had not a courier pounded up on a lathered horse and given a sealed document to the officer in charge just as the officer's saber was falling in the traditional signal and the squad's fingers were tightening on their triggers. Our friend was then escorted over the border and set free. He must have told the story to a lot of people; it kept coming out later in book plots.

The Swiss further endeared himself to Sid and me by taking the two of us on camping expeditions into the hills, where we cooked our own bacon and baked potatoes by burying them in the ground and building a fire over them. He gave us each a .22 rifle. Sid's was a single-shot Stevens and mine was a fancy semi-automatic Remington with a barrel bent just enough to make bullets go in interesting trajectories. With the rifles he gave us a handful of cartridges.

All fired up with war stories, one day Sid and I went out behind the tent-house, dug what were perhaps the first scientific foxholes in modern military history, and next day, when we had made sure nobody was around, we had ourselves a war.

Piling loose dirt in front of our holes, which were twenty or thirty yards apart, we stuck lengths of two-inch iron pipe through the dirt for firing ports, and began shooting over each other's heads. The bullets made a fine ripping sound when they struck the top of the breastworks and ricocheted. It was a foolish business, and it ended when I forgot about my crooked gun barrel. I tried to shoot a rock off the top of Sid's dirt pile and knock it in on top of him, but I put the bullet into his pipe. Fortunately, he was not looking through it at the moment.

There came a frightened howl from the enemy trench, I suspended fire, we had a shaky parley under truce, and the war was over.

But we learned a fundamental bit of strategy from this —how to keep an enemy pinned down by fire—which came in handy when we started going to the desert school. The schoolhouse was a one-room frame affair, with a single teacher for eight grades. The schoolyard equipment consisted only of two privies and a large planked table with benches, where the kids ate their lunches. We were a rugged lot of little prairie wolves, toughened by desert life, and we had a great deal of energy. For a while we divided into teams and had rockfights, with several of the girls participating.

One team would upend the table and use it as a barricade; the other team would try to take the fort. Sid and I

always joined the attackers and constantly won, because half the attackers would keep rocks humming about the table, forcing the defenders to keep their heads in and lob aimless missiles high over at us. The falling rocks had no force at all—we were often hit on the head and shoulders and had only minor scratches from it. The other half of the attackers would crawl to the heavy table in perfect safety and push it over on the defenders. Then we'd plaster them as they scattered. The very ease of the game made it boring after a while, and we took up tame sports like football, in which a rock was carried by the runner. The instant a runner had the "ball," the entire pack, including his own team, turned on him and dumped him.

There were four or five pupils in each grade. Mrs. Hill, our amiable but harried teacher, had her hands full. I was nine at the time and was entitled to be a fourth-grader, but Mrs. Hill jumped me to the fifth grade. She claimed it was because I read a lot, but I've always believed it was because she wanted to keep some symmetry in the classroom. The fourth grade was overloaded and the fifth had only a lonely couple, including Mrs. Hill's daughter Lucile, a very striking little blonde who never played our rough games and was a perfect lady in every respect.

Lucile brought out the best in me: I fell in love with her at the same time Sid had his first big affair of the heart.

Sid, a tall, skinny kid with a pleasant and rather handsome face and an amiable way about him, got Josephine on his personal merits, while Lucile, as she herself later admitted to me, took up with me because I could draw Duesenberg cars.

Josephine had a very lovely face and an extremely plump figure. She was almost a head taller than my brother and outweighed him by a good ninety pounds. I still have a picture to prove it. I used to rag my brother about his romance, accusing him of wanting a bodyguard rather than a sweetheart. When they were together he looked like her shadow. But she was devoted to him, and was a very sweet person.

From time to time the whole community went off on picnics to the mountains or to one of the cool, green spots on the desert where the water level was near the surface. Traveling in convoy to and from the picnics was as much fun as the parties themselves, what with everybody riding in someone else's car or truck and singing and jabbering and pelting jack rabbits beside the road. We went on one of these picnics shortly after the beginning of Sid's and my love affairs, and of course the two girls went along. Sid and I cleverly maneuvered ourselves into riding in the same cars with our respective ladies.

I remember these early romances had corrupted both Sid and me to such an extent that the night before the picnic we wetted and slicked down our hair, which tended to be very stiff and unruly, and slept with stocking-caps, made of an old pair of our mother's hose, pulled tightly over our ears, so that next morning we were quite dudish.

During the long ride Lucile and I held hands all the way; she seemed in a very affectionate mood, and I hoped that when we reached the picnic ground she and I could sort of disappear into the wilds together. But when we arrived at the chosen spot—an abandoned copper mine high in a range of mountains some forty miles from our homestead—Lucile disengaged herself from me and stuck close by her mother, ignoring the cow-eyes I made at her.

At the mine there was a well that had once fed a concrete reservoir, which now contained an inch or two of rain water. There were hundreds of frogs around both the well and the reservoir, and most of the kids sharpened sticks and joyfully started chasing and killing the creatures while the grownups greased skillets for fried frog-legs. This seemed a brutal activity to me at the moment—my heart was softened by love—and for want of anything better to do I trailed after Sid and his big sweetheart, who were doing exactly what I'd wanted to do with Lucile: they were rambling up a long ravine in the mountainside.

They were quite friendly when they saw me and invited me to walk with them. A splendid couple, I began to realize—far above silly necking and cooing. Theirs was a deep, abiding affection which required no sloppy demonstrations.

At one point the sides of the ravine formed rather steep cliffs thirty feet high. Sid saw a cliff which promised hand and foot holds all the way up, and started to climb it.

"Don't do it, Sid," Josephine protested, wisely, for while the rocky cliff looked solid, it was shale, which is very loose and treacherous stuff.

"Aw, I've climbed lots worse things than this. Ask Billy about some of the places I've climbed at Mountain Park. Huh, Billy?"

"Yeh, sure," I lied, "we used to go up big cliffs together, tied together with a long rope so if one of us fell the other one could catch him."

"That's right. This little ol' cliff is nothing."

"All right, let Billy climb it," said Josephine, making it plain what she thought of me. But Sid felt adventuresome and went on up, getting within two feet of the top when his handhold gave way and he came crashing down, bringing a cascade of shale with him. He hit the creek bed all crumpled up and out cold.

Josephine screamed loudly, pounced on him, picked up his poor, broken body, and carried him, as if he'd been a doll, back toward the picnic grounds. I shuffled along behind, very upset and worried. We hadn't gone far when some awful thing came over me, I don't know what, and I burst out laughing in a most obnoxiously loud voice. I

have always liked to think since then that it was hysteria from worry about Sid, not ribaldry at the sight of that huge, fine figure of a girl carrying my big brother so lightly and gently.

She turned her head with dignity and threw such a look of terrible disgust at me that it shamed me into silence for a moment—then I was off again, howling with mirth. When my Pop met us halfway back to the picnic grounds, having heard the scream and starting a frantic search for us, he saw Josephine carrying what looked like the corpse of his eldest son, all bloody and mashed, and followed by a little squirt who was hollering his head off with mad laughter. He must have had a terrible jolt.

Back at the picnic grounds Sid recovered consciousness. He was surrounded by worried people, bandaged tenderly, and propped like a wounded warrior against a tree. He had sprained his back and ankle, cracked a couple of ribs, and cut himself in numerous places. The whole picnic began to revolve about him: people sang to him, choice morsels were brought to him, and several boys loaded him into an old ore car, which was still perched on its tiny tracks, and pushed him wherever he wanted to go. I wanted to help push, but they wouldn't let me near my brother.

And all the time Sid's girl kept going around and saying, "Billy made him climb up there. I tried to stop him but Billy egged him on."

She warned me not to get within arm's reach or she'd smash me like a tarantula. My own Lucile wouldn't even speak to me. And for weeks afterward I would sometimes catch my Pop peering at me from the corner of his eye—

not angrily, but wonderingly, as if I might have crawled out of a Charles Addams cartoon.

An unexpected and welcome source of income came to the desert at a time when Pop's pocket, as well as the pockets of several other family men, was getting very empty. A gentleman of means, afflicted with tuberculosis, arrived in the desert from the Middle West, bringing his family. He wanted a large house built of desert rock, a yard landscaped about it, a well dug, and a pump installed.

A dozen homesteaders, including Pop, got the job of building the house, at a fairly good wage. It took only a few weeks because rocks were plentiful, good materials were hauled in from Phoenix, and all the workers were skillful with their hands and experienced in different phases of building. While the house was going up, the owners occasionally drove out from their hotel suite in Phoenix to watch, and Sid and I, who often hung around the construction, made friends with the ailing man's eldest son, who was about our age. His charm was enhanced, to us, by an announcement he made, for no reason we could see, because we'd been talking about something else, on the very first day of our acquaintance.

"I got sixty dollars, all my own, in the bank."

Sid and I were not strangers to affluence, for we had

each owned a small bronze bank, shaped like a book, into which Christmas quarters and half dollars from parents and relatives had gone. Our banks had, at one time, accumulated the magnificent total of about five dollars apiece, but recently we had started looting them, and very little was left. We felt, somehow instinctively, that if we kept close to this boy who was almost a millionaire, some of his wealth might rub off and attach itself to us. It was a futile hope; we should have known that anyone with the brains to collect sixty dollars so early in life was not going to part with it easily.

One day during this period I overheard my mother, who was in some ways a hypochondriac where Sid and I were concerned, talking with Pop about this new friendship.

"Sidney, do you think it's wise to let them play with a boy whose father has t.b.?"

I hadn't thought one way or another about it before—I wasn't even sure what tuberculosis was. But I promptly took pains to find out. The results horrified me. Every person I asked during the next few days had a different theory about consumption and its contagious qualities. Some said that if a t.b. victim so much as touched a doorknob, it was deadly to handle it for years afterwards.

I developed a morbid horror of diseases from this. I was sure Sid and I were goners, having even drunk from the same cup as a boy who lived right in the same house, and probably even ate from the same dishes, with an afflicted father, and that it was only a matter of time until our insides dropped out and our brains melted.

I became very sanitary, washing my hands frequently during the day, inspecting my tongue for signs of decay, and breaking into a cold sweat every time I woke up during the night with a dry throat or an arm numb from

having been slept on. Sid was blissfully unaware of his doom. I had considerately spared him the facts and was suffering alone.

While I was in this state of mind, a new terror came up. Another of those big community picnics was planned, this time at one of the desert's natural little green oases about ten miles from our place. When we arrived at the picnic, I found myself closely inspecting our neighbors' physical aspects, which before I had pretty well taken for granted. They were a perfectly normal collection of adults, with average blemishes. Now, every skin defect or stooped shoulder, every bloodshot eye, every twitch of the hands, became a subject for my critical examination. I went from person to person, staring at each one from top to toe, until finally I became rather conspicuous and several people got annoyed with me.

The children, all of whom I knew, were also an average-looking lot, with perhaps a bit more tanned sturdiness than would be found in a group of city kids. But they looked a sickly and contagious bunch to me that day, and I refrained from horsing around with them while they climbed trees and threw rocks. People began commenting to my parents that something seemed wrong with me; a lady suggested that perhaps I should wear a hat in the sun.

For the first time I observed that a friend of Pop's, whom I'd seen frequently at our house and at the store, had the forefinger missing from his right hand. I was appalled that I hadn't noticed it before. I knew it was bad manners to stare, but I couldn't keep my eyes from his hand. During the half hour before lunch, while the ladies were spreading the food around and the men sat under trees and talked, I sat near this fellow and gawked at him until finally he caught me at it. Good naturedly, he dangled his hand before my face, causing me to recoil violently.

"Tell you how this happened, Billy," he said. "It rotted off."

"H-how?" I gulped, shaken.

"Used to have a job setting out cabbage," he explained. "Some fellas use tools to make the holes for the little plants, so their fingers won't get wrinkled and sore from the wet ground. But I always used my finger to make the holes. I was a youngster then, full of vinegar, and I figured my finger was tougher than any tool. Well, after a while, it just rotted off."

This brought a general chuckle at my expense, but I was greatly relieved to find the finger hadn't gone as a result of some disease, and until lunchtime I stayed close to the man, feeling he was less infectious than anybody else. I ate carefully, staying away from such things as pickles and olives, where strange hands had been poking around.

After lunch, feeling somewhat better, and more fortified against bacteria, I joined the younger set in an expedition to a deserted two-room shack nearby. We played around in it, climbed on the roof, smashed the one remaining pane of glass in the windows, and poked around under the house with long sticks, hoping to dislodge a snake we could kill.

Tiring of the play after a bit, I went back to the cluster of men—who were again smoking and making talk under the trees—just in time to hear one of them begin reminiscing about the family that had lived in the deserted house.

It couldn't have been worse. The family's only daughter had been stricken with something called "spinamennagitis." People who live in remote places tend to love morbid talk and since no one present was too well informed on medical lore, the discussion on "spinamennagitis" was enough to curl anyone's hair.

"She was a real pretty little girl," the fellow said. "Big eyes and curly hair, and smart too. Used to read all the time. Her mother used to say she wished they had a piano or something because the kid liked music and maybe had a knack for it."

"Poor little tyke," said somebody else.

"You should have seen her afterwards. I was over at their house three-four times while she was sick. One of her legs got brittle. I swear you could have blowed on it and it would've snapped off."

"You don't say."

"Things started happening fast. First she went blind and couldn't read no more, and with that stiff leg she couldn't sleep so good, so her folks stayed up all night and read to her."

There were signs of moisture appearing in several eyes.

"Then she got deaf and dumb, and it wasn't no good to talk to her or anything. She just laid there and suffered. There's no telling what went on in that kid's mind, all shut off like that from everything. Then one night that leg broke off. They buried it behind the house, and had a regular little funeral over it."

"You don't say!"

Looking over at the shack, I saw my friends still playing in it, and I felt like crying for them. Already scheduled to die of t.b., I wasn't quite so frightened for myself, until the thought struck me that the "spinamennagitis," which sounded infinitely worse than consumption, might get me first. A breeze came up, blowing from the shack toward us. I think the only reason I didn't begin sprinting across the desert to avoid the millions of airborne germs was because nobody else was running. If my leg was going to break off, at least I would have plenty of company hobbling about, and that was a great comfort.

One moonlit night not long after the picnic we drove home from a visit with the Robinsons along the road past the same deserted shack. I tried, unsuccessfully, to avoid

looking at the house. Its empty windows stared blackly at me, and I had visions of the stricken child moaning inside. When we got home at nine p.m., I asked my parents

if I could take a bath. I think I was beginning to frighten
them a little.

Late one afternoon, not many weeks after the big flood
on the desert, there came one of those bits of weather
which residents of the Florida Keys have learned to dread.
The whole earth seemed to stop moving and breathing,
and for the first time the dry Arizona air seemed close
and sticky. The horizon looked muddy—I can't exactly
describe it, but it had a heavy, leaden look. A wind came
up just before dusk.

Pop's past travels had taken him out of our little world
of the Southwest, and he had either seen at first hand or
heard tales of hurricanes.

"It doesn't seem natural to me that there'd be a hurricane out here," he said, but as the wind stiffened and
began moaning a bit, he figured that we were in for at
least a good imitation of a heavy blow. Hurriedly he
briefed Sid and me.

"This place hasn't got any foundations, and if the wind
catches it broadside it'll blow us all over the map. Roll up
those flaps all the way around so it'll blow through the
screens."

We rolled up the canvas blinds and immediately the
sheets flew from the beds and, in company with several

towels from the washstand, plastered themselves against the far screen.

Pop made his way out to the privy, leaning heavily into the wind and staggering now and then when a gust caught him. He ripped off the El Toro cement bags so the light

framework, which had already started shivering excitedly, wouldn't take off. The wind struck with real fury while he was coming back, bowling him over so violently he almost somersaulted. He came the rest of the way on his hands and knees, while we howled with glee and yelled "Yay, Pop!" and rooted for him, while huddled down in the protection of the three-foot-high walls, with only our eyes and the tops of our heads showing. Our hair stood out straight, like wind-socks at an airport. Pop didn't come in immediately—crawling around on his knees and occasionally standing up when he had an especially heavy object in his hands, he tugged and pulled rocks, bits of junk from his "spare parts" pile, and all the pieces of wood he could find to the windward side of the house, to break the wind somewhat and prevent a gust from getting under us and lifting the whole house. I'm sure it was the only thing that saved the place.

When he finally made his way to the door the wind had become frightful: it screamed, it howled, it buffeted. The instant Pop opened the door it was torn out of his hands and off its hinges, and we watched it sail gracefully away like a kite, high in the air. (We found it later in a Palo Verde tree, almost a mile away. I don't know how the tree was able to catch and hold it.)

We were glad to have Pop inside with us: not so much for his company as for the added ballast. We needed it badly. Frequently the house would be lifted bodily at one corner or another, hesitate a second while we all blanched, then settle back on its base.

"I'm a damn fool," Pop grunted to himself. "Should have brought all that heavy junk inside to hold us down instead of piling it outside. Even a couple crankshafts and a cylinder head would weigh a good hundred pounds and might make just enough difference to keep us from blowing away."

In our opinion Pop had acted bravely and intelligently,

as if hurricanes were an everyday thing with him, and we told him so. It seemed to please him.

All through the night we hugged the floor and listened to flying pebbles and bits of brush smack the side of the house and watched fearfully while the wind, sometimes blowing with a steady howl like a fire siren and sometimes growing fitful and dying for a moment before hitting us like a huge fist, shredded our canvas roof and snatched the scraps away so quickly we couldn't see them go. Perhaps the torn roof did as much as anything else to save the place, for with the wind moving through it and through the screen sides, our wall presented only a three-foot-high surface. I think I must have slept from time to time because I don't remember some of the things that happened, such as the rabbit which Pop swore came through the air like a bird and was flattened on our wall.

Early in the morning the wind suddenly died to a breeze. It's a wonder the entire desert, which had braced itself all night against the wall of air, didn't fall on its face. We went outside to look around and were surprised that things still were more or less in their proper places. Our pet Palo Verde tree looked sagged and naked, and our ancient ironwood had lost a number of its branches. Any tree less flexible than the former, or less firmly rooted and low in silhouette than the latter, would have been uprooted. Our privy framework, even without its cement-bag sails, had been carried away. Great piles of brush were stacked against the house, which was a mess, and against the truck, which had somehow stayed in one position.

We were full of high spirits; we still had a house and

could always find more canvas for the roof. Our next thought was for our neighbors. We set out in the truck to see how they'd fared, finding that the roads, which at best had been no more than paths cleared through the greasewood, had completely disappeared in spots, the wind having filled the old ruts with dirt and sand and pebbles.

The first place we came to, six or eight miles away, belonged to a homesteader family that had recently built a nice little three- or four-room frame cottage, a chicken house where they kept a dozen hens, and a doghouse. As we approached the place we remembered they'd gone East for a visit and had paid a man from Litchfield to come out and feed the chickens and the dog and keep an eye on things.

Physicists say that a tightly closed, fragile-walled structure is in danger of "exploding" in certain types of high winds. Apparently the outside pressure changes constantly during the blow, and the inside pressure sometimes can't keep up with the change quickly enough. When the pressure drops to a partial vacuum outside, the normal air inside pushes the walls out. That's what must have happened to this place, for the house, the chicken house, and the doghouse had vanished. All that remained was a litter of boards and broken furniture. When we pulled up, appalled at the sight, we noticed the hired man sitting unhappily on the edge of the house floor, which had actually been shifted some yards. The fellow was holding his foot and muttering obscenities.

"I seen there was a big wind blowin' up," he told us, "and I shut up the chickens so they wouldn't get blowed away, I shut up the dog so he wouldn't start whinin' around, and I went in the house and shut it up tight so dirt wouldn't blow all over everything. I even shut the damper on the stove pipe so nothing would come in it.

I went to sleep on my cot in the kitchen, and when I woke up there was the most God-awful clatter and crashing, and the house had gone. I was layin' on the kitchen floor all bloodied up. I'd tangled with my ax somehow—it was leaning on the wall. Look at my foot."

He took his hands away from his instep, and I remember my heart started pounding very hard, for I'd never seen a gash like that. The ax had almost split his foot in two, several little white bones were showing, and for the first time I noticed big splotches of blood all over the floor.

Pop fancied himself as a rather expert amateur doctor. He had a painless method, when Sid or I had a loose tooth, of twisting molars out with his thumb and forefinger, and a ritual always followed whereby we'd put the tooth under a pillow at night and wake up to find a dime in its place.

With an air of professional confidence he examined the foot and found that while the ax had cut a lot of meat it had not severed any bones. He found a roll of gauze bandage in the litter of the kitchen, bandaged the foot tightly, put the man in our truck, and we took a last quick look around the wreckage before taking him home for further treatment.

There wasn't a chicken in sight. Presumably the wind, after blowing their house away, had plucked them up and carried them off bodily. If they could have been found their flight would probably have set an all-time record for long-distance migration of domestic fowl. The dog sat right where his house had been, in a state of considerable shock. The doghouse, which had had no floor and no fastenings, had been yanked from over his head sometime during the night. We tried to call him to us so we could take him home, but he only stared belligerently at us. Obviously he intended to stay right there without budging until that goddam wind brought his house back and put it down where it belonged.

In the middle of a welter of bedding, furniture, and boards were the remains of a medium-size cast-iron cookstove which had been thrown, rocked, buffeted, and smashed to pieces. Right beside this evidence of the mighty power of the storm was one of those very thin and fragile glass chimneys from a kerosene lamp. A husky mouse can almost break one of those chimneys by kicking it, yet this one was perfectly intact. No hurricane or cyclone story is complete without its phenomena angle: straws driven into trees and roosters whirled into gallon jugs. I feel duty-bound to record the lamp chimney and the stove.

On the way home in the truck with the casualty Pop kept pursing his lips and blowing through his nose, and we knew he was figuring a way to doctor the poor fellow.

By the time we got home, his remedy had been decided upon. We had a largish bottle of iodine in a chest. It was almost full. Pop took off the bandage and poured the entire contents of the bottle into the man's open wound.

I remember the words well, but I can't repeat them here. I have never in my life, not even in five years of the army, heard such swearing. It was like a string of Chinese firecrackers going off. Pop's victim, who'd seemed very weak from loss of blood, showed an amazing vitality, hopping about in great leaps on one foot, clutching the other with both hands, his face contorted weirdly, screaming such awful oaths at my Pop and questioning his ancestry with such bitterness and sincerity that we'd all have been offended under different circumstances.

The fellow yelled in agony and hopped and groaned and rolled on the ground and carried on for so long that Pop finally became a little worried. He'd planned to put the poor man in bed and take us out again to visit our other neighbors and help them, as we'd helped this one. But now Pop carried him to the truck, put him back in the cab, and took him to Litchfield to see a doctor. Pop came back several hours later, and he seemed strangely and grimly quiet when we questioned him. It took a long time to drag his story out; it seems that the doctor's cussing when he saw what had happened had almost topped the casualty's profanity. The doctor had assumed considerable authority and had, in a most highhanded way, revoked Pop's license to practice medicine in the state of Arizona, and had warned him that jail was the best he could expect should the victim's foot be amputated as a result of the iodine burns in an otherwise neat wound, which would have required only washing and stitching. Evidently the man recovered; nothing more was heard from him.

Everybody's place was in a shambles from the wind. Not all the houses had blown down, but ours was the only one in a fourteen-mile radius that needed only minor repairs. For many days Pop was kept busy repaying all the neighbors who'd so generously helped us build our own house. He went from place to place, nailing, looking for

lumber, bolting, sawing, and giving advice on everything
but first aid.

My mother got along well with everybody on the
desert. She had inherited a very kind and warm heart from
her own mother; no matter how bad things were with us,
she could always find someone in worse shape, and she
could always find something of ours to give them. Sid and
I learned not to become too attached to a pair of pants or
a shirt—we'd put an article of clothing away, planning to
use it a week later, and within a remarkably short time
we'd find somebody else's kid wearing it. This could be
infuriating sometimes. She was even worse about her own
things. There were times when Pop would want to take
us to a party somewhere and would find she'd given away
her only fancy dress.

Pop was very generous too, but he would cover it up
with bluster. Sometimes he showed a real temper, and
when he was hot about something he would make the most
terrible threats and say pretty extravagant things—about
killings and feuds and so on. This used to impress Sid and
me strongly. We kept asking Pop how many men he'd
killed during the war, and he kept giving us the stock
answer all war veterans, as I've learned since, give their
kids:

"Well, son, in modern war you seldom see the enemy up close. There's always a lot of shooting going on, and nobody ever knows who killed who."

This covers a multitude of sins; the answer is good whether a man hustled rations in a rear-area depot or was a machine gunner. In the case of the former, the kid is left with the impression that his father is a very mysterious and modest fellow; with the latter, the father, who knows damned well he killed a lot of people, doesn't want to fill his kid with gory thoughts, and finds the reply a convenient evasion. Actually, my own Pop was an artilleryman.

When Pop was sore at somebody and began stewing around and talking of violence, Sid and I were always encouraging about it. Once we almost got him in trouble. Sometime during the general repair work after the hurricane he developed a feud with a homesteader, came home, started cleaning his pistol, and muttering.

"Be doing the world a favor shooting such a louse."

I think the argument had started about roads: on the way to the store we sometimes took a route which crossed the enemy's property. He'd allegedly passed a low remark, about people who trespass, to some friend of Pop's and the friend had duly reported it.

"He don't deserve a quick death. I'll let him have it in the gut."

More cleaning of the gun. Much frowning and squinting through the barrel. A little oil on the slide and on each side of the hammer.

"Bastard thinks he owns the desert."

Gun stuck under belt. No good. Gun placed in hip pocket with butt showing.

"I got a good mind to go over to that shiftless mutt's house and make him crawl."

Full of loyalty and enthusiasm, Sid and I egged Pop on, and he let us prod him far past the point where he should have stopped talking. Finally, he was faced with the choice of going through with his threats or of looking foolish to his kids. So he set out in the truck with the pistol. Sid and I were determined to go with him; he naturally refused to let us, so we waited till he'd driven off and then followed on foot.

It was a long way; it took us almost two hours to get to our enemy's house, and we approached it in a state of great excitement, chills running up our backs when we saw Pop's truck standing beside the house. There was no sign of life, and three terrible thoughts hit us in rapid succession. What if they'd both fired at once and were both dead? What if the dirty skunk had seen Pop coming and had ambushed him from behind a greasewood bush? What if Pop had won the fight but would go to prison? We were feeling a little sick by the time we got close enough to see

Pop sitting on the fellow's front doorstep, smoking nervously, the pistol still in his hip pocket. He looked terribly relieved when he saw us come up, all footsore and unhappy, and he bundled us into the truck and took us back to our house.

Nobody had been home when he had driven over to "feud," he told us, and he had been waiting for the man to come back, at which time he'd planned to give the fellow fair warning and plenty of time to get his own gun before starting to throw lead. No low-down bushwhacker, *our* Pop—he was a fair fighter, which was more than we could say for his enemy, probably.

I've often wondered what would have happened if the fellow had been home when Pop drove up. Possibly somebody would have been hurt—on the other hand, possibly not. Two weeks later I saw them drinking together from a glass jug at Winter's Well.

The little black "Boston Terrier," which we'd bought in Mexico for a dollar and which was with us constantly for twelve years until he died of a throat infection brought on by a jagged chicken bone, has not figured in my accounts of minor and major adventures on the Arizona desert, because he seemed a homebody. He would have none of our gold mines or snake hunts or dynamite caps;

he seemed to prefer to spend his days around the house watching my mother do her chores of cooking and cleaning for the screwball males of the tribe.

In fact, we became a little worried about him. He had done nothing spectacular since he'd bitten off the end of

my brother's nose, and we felt his lassitude was due to loneliness. We needn't have worried. We found out, after some months in Arizona, that his quietness during the day was due to the fact that every night, after we'd gone to sleep, he trekked miles across the desert to the house of a tubercular lady. Our dog was carrying on with her dog, a Scotty bitch, who evidently gave Blackie a high old time of it, for he was out almost every night.

But he was a smart seducer. Toward the end of our stay on the homestead, he actually had *her* coming over to *our* house every night. And he made such a tramp of her that when her mistress finally pulled up stakes and went back East, the Scotty didn't go along. Her mistress, who loved the little trollop dearly, hunted and called for her, we found later, until right up to the time she had to leave to make her train in Phoenix. All the time her dog had been at our place.

We found the lady's new address and wrote her, offering to ship the dog express collect, but we never got an answer. So it came about that we found ourselves the owners of two parent dogs and a litter of young ones. Becoming a father seemed to do something to Blackie. He perked up considerably, made a fresh pass at Sid's nose and almost got mine once or twice, and he started making little expeditions into the desert, skipping around from greasewood to greasewood, wagging his rear end (he had no tail at all —not even a stump) at the contents of each bush, and yapping delightedly as if to say, "Where has this wonderful desert been all my life?"

One day, while his children were still very tiny, he went out and captured himself a Gila monster. The Gila (pronounced heela) is a gorgeous reptile found in Mexico and in parts of our Southwest. He's a big lizard, extremely poisonous, averaging about eighteen inches in length. His hide, made up of tiny orange and black beads in pretty groups and patterns, looks like the product of a handicraft class at a boys' summer camp. Gila monsters are bashful about making public appearances; they are also sluggish and surly in temperament.

Our pooch had cornered this specimen in a greasewood a few hundred yards from the house and was handling him

with great intelligence. Like rattlers, Gilas can't stand the desert sun, and every time this one would try to break out of his shady bush and start for his hole, the dog would let him get a little way out into the sun, then bedevil and confuse him and force him back into the bush, all the while barking and yapping to attract us to the scene. By the time we located the source of the commotion, ran back to the house, got a box, and secured the Gila, the reptile was pretty subdued.

The box was about twenty inches long, and it wasn't until we got our prize into it and nailed a piece of screen over him that we realized he was a very big Gila. His tail was cramped and bent, and he could hardly move in the box. He was at least twenty-four inches long. We wondered what to do with him—had he been a rattler we'd have killed him promptly, but this creature, despite the fact that he was deadly venomous, seemed much too pretty to rub out.

The same evening, Pop went to Winter's Well, where he happened to mention our big catch, and somebody told him that a zoo in the East had once paid four thousand dollars for a twenty-three-inch Gila, then thought to be the largest ever seen. Ours was at least an inch longer. Pop returned all excited; we moved our precious captive into a bigger and more comfortable crate, and next morning Pop almost burned out a bearing racing into Phoenix with the crate on the truck seat beside him.

In Phoenix Pop found that supply exceeded demand in the Gila monster market. Not only could he not get four thousand dollars for ours from a zoo; he couldn't even get forty cents for it at one of those roadside ptomaine traps which entice tourists with the sign "See the Fabulous Desert Creatures—the Greatest Collection in Captivity." They were all loaded with Gilas.

But Pop was never one to waste a trip. Determined to spend some money if he couldn't make any and having animals on his mind, he bought a nanny goat in Phoenix. When he returned to the desert with a large white goat curled up on the seat of the truck cab beside him and the Gila monster in its box on the floor, our first inclination was to smell his breath. This we did, taking turns, my mother first, then Sid, then me. Not only was his breath pure, but he had an explanation for the goat:

"On the way to town I was figuring what we could do with four thousand shekels. I got to thinking about the sprouts. They've been getting plenty to eat and a lot of sun but they've been looking a little peaked lately and I got to thinking maybe it was fresh milk they needed.

"I look down at this Gila on the seat by me and I says 'You're gonna buy a couple of cows you damn spotted lizard I says and you're gonna buy a couple of wells, too, so we can raise alfalfa.' The Gila looks at me with those mean little eyes and doesn't say anything back.

"Well when there wasn't any Gila sale I says to myself there's no reason why the sprouts can't have milk anyway so I think what's next to a cow and I know it's a goat. A nanny goat would be easy to feed and will put out plenty of milk for the sprouts and besides I know for a fact that that goat milk is healthier than cow milk."

This made some sense. And the goat was a honey, as we found out within a few minutes after her arrival. We named her Nanny. (We were never noted for great originality in naming our livestock; it's a real wonder we never called any of our dogs Rover.) We tested her product right away, and were surprised to find that Pop was a good goat-chooser, for she gave a great quantity of sweet milk, only slightly drier in taste than cow milk.

We were so busy examining the new addition to our household that we forgot all about the Gila monster, whose crate had been taken from the truck and set in the shade at one side of the house. When we did think of him several hours later, we voted unanimously that, since he was worthless as a financial asset and had been the instrument which had brought us our Nanny, he deserved a chance at life like anybody else, and we decided to take him far out into a nonpopulated part of the desert and set him free. Unhappily, several hours had passed, the sun had moved and had taken the shadow with it, and the Gila had been in its blaze for the better part of an hour with nothing but the screen above him. He was dead as a doornail. Not too regretfully (although we were sorry it had not been a more merciful death) we buried him, very deep.

But not deep enough. A week later he was spotted, dug up, and eaten by an alert Airedale that belonged to a neighbor—the Olsens, I think. I never had much respect for the pooch afterward. A dog that will eat a ripe Gila monster will eat anything. It's a wonder it didn't kill him. The Airedale was evidently not welcomed home, for he hung around our place, stinking to high heaven and burping and retching, and whining, for weeks afterwards, a lonely, bloated, and pitiful outcast. No human could come within fifty yards of him. Sid or I would place a pan of food for him some hundred yards away and then run like the devil before he could come up to thank us.

The stuff about goats eating tin cans is nonsense, but Nanny did have queer tastes. We used to throw our dishwater out into the wash, where the dry sand in the bottom would soak up the soapy water instantly. The very afternoon Nanny joined us we threw out the supper dishwater in the usual manner and were surprised to see her bound to the spot where it had disappeared and start licking furiously at the sand.

When night fell, we wondered where to bed her down.

She showed a strong preference for the house, running in and jumping on the big bed every time the door was opened, but of course that wouldn't do. She finally settled on the seat in the truck cab and went happily to sleep.

Next morning, before throwing out the breakfast dishwater, we decided to let Nanny have a sniff at the pan, to see if perhaps it was the smell of soap that attracted her. She buried her muzzle deep in the pan and while we watched, somewhat startled, she began sucking the contents up at a great speed. Pop tried to pull the pan away; she hooked her chin stubbornly over the edge, wiggled her horns menacingly, finished the last drop, and began licking up the bits of froth clinging to the edges.

We milked her, of course, for the man who'd sold her had told Pop she must be milked twice daily. But we threw it away without tasting it, and put out a pan of fresh drinking water, hoping that the soapy stuff would have passed through her by the time she was ready for her evening contribution. All through the day, even though she became so thirsty by midafternoon that her tongue protruded slightly between her teeth, she stubbornly refused the good water, and nosed about our outdoor kitchen, sometimes rearing on her hind legs, trying to reach the cake of kitchen soap which had been placed on a high shelf.

In desperation, afraid she'd die of thirst, we finally gave in, and let her have the dishwater again. The creature drank until her sides swelled alarmingly, then begged for more. When the evening milking came, we tested her product gingerly, each of us taking only a tiny sip, in the faint hope that the soap had perhaps worked out through her skin or something before it had hit the milk factory. We found the milk hadn't been affected at all—if anything, it was sweeter than it had been the night before.

From then on Nanny got all the dishwater. She wanted our bath water, too (we bathed in a large galvanized-iron clothes tub), but we had a conference about that and decided it would be terribly unsanitary to drink milk whose chief ingredient would be water we'd washed in. On the other hand, we comforted ourselves, there was nothing really wrong with dishwater, for that had only been used for plates and utensils which had contained substance already proved edible. In fact, Nanny's liking for dishwater was a very good thing on the desert, considering the cost and trouble of getting a barrelful—it meant the same water was used twice.

Pop and his mining partner Pat enjoyed drinking lustily, and perhaps it was fortunate that their means seldom permitted full indulgence in their desires. The fact that prohibition was on meant little to most homesteaders—store-bought liquor would have been too expensive anyway—and each man had his own recipe for various beverages. Pop and Pat made a potent home-brew beer which many of their friends swore had more kick than most bootleg bourbons and gins. The stuff was mixed in a five-gallon crock and allowed to age until somebody was thirsty. Although they used the term "beer," the ingredients changed from batch to batch, and sometimes the brew's only kinship to beer was in the fact that it foamed vigorously when disturbed.

The only place in our one-room house where the crock wouldn't be disturbed too much or knocked over was on the floor at the end of the little bench which we used as a washstand, and on which stood a tin basin and a saucer holding a cake of soap. The crock was always covered with a large tin lid which overlapped the sides. One day, shortly after Nanny had joined the family, I accidentally broke the soapdish. There happened to be a shortage of saucers at the moment, so the soap was just left on the bare bench, pending the time when we'd remember to get a new dish for it. A fresh brew had been "aging" for several days in the crock, and, during the evening of the day I broke the soapdish Pop and Pat had tested a quart or two

to see if the mixture was "ready," and had accidentally forgotten to replace the crock's cover.

How the soap got into the brew nobody knows. I was subsequently blamed for it, I suppose because I'd broken the saucer, but I've always suspected that two men careless enough, or exhilarated enough by their "testing," to leave the cover off a crock of delicate liquid could have, with equal carelessness, knocked the soap in. It took them two days and two gallons of further "testing" before they got down to the soapy-tasting part. By that time the soap had pretty well dissolved and worked its way upward.

It seemed a shame, but Pop and Pat, after feeling around in the bottom of the crock and contacting the last soft lump of soap remaining, decided the brew had to go. Pop was about to carry the crock out and dump it when Pat came up with a devilish idea: Nanny liked soapy water; why wouldn't she love soapy beer?

My mother and Sid and I had driven to the store and didn't return until just after Nanny had drunk the two gallons of contaminated joy-juice and polished off the tiny lump of soap sticking to the bottom of the crock. Her sides were distended; already she was beginning to lurch. As we got out of the truck Nanny looked blearily at us and greeted us with a drunken gabble. Then she walked toward us with her body at an angle so oblique to her course that she was going almost sideways. She began blowing frothy bubbles and reeking of stale beer, reminding us, in a way, of the poor Airedale who'd consumed the Gila monster.

It was a very wild afternoon. My mother was in a state; she was so furious she threatened to sic the ASPCA on Nanny's bartenders. Sid and I were equally upset. We thought a lot of the goat. Pop and Pat were feeling very abashed, although somewhat tipsy—either they'd helped Nanny finish the brew or had found something else. The only person who seemed to be enjoying herself completely was Nanny, and she was so ludicrous that after a while we couldn't help getting a little hysterical.

The goat was full of affection for everyone; she tried to climb into our laps, and at one stage she became very coy and flirtatious with Pop. She would come up to him, bat her huge eyes rapidly, and mumble goat-talk through her frothy whiskers. When Pop, with tears of remorse and laughter in his eyes, would reach out to pat her gently on the head and tell her everything was going to be all right, she would dance away from him, at that same oblique angle she had used when first greeting us. Then she would grin at him and invite him to try it again.

The effects of the beer did not diminish as time went on —she seemed to get tighter, in fact, and her angle of movement increased to the point where she walked completely sideways, miraculously untangling her feet and not falling down once. When milking time came we had a real problem; she wouldn't let the family come near her, except on her own terms. When someone reached for her teats she became positively outraged. Her attitude seemed to be, as each of us approached her in turn, that the fact that she loved us dearly did not mean she was going to let anyone take such intimate liberties with a lady in her cups.

It got on toward dusk; we forgot about our own supper and became very worried about the milking problem. Finally Pat, who heretofore had not tried to approach the reeling goat, made a suggestion:

"Maybe I can hannle 'er. A 'runk goat might unnerstan' a 'runk man."

So Pat took the bucket in hand, and sure enough, Nanny let him come to her. Unfortunately, we forgot to brief Pat on procedure until it was too late. He had never milked a goat before. Now, we milked Nanny from her right side, as a cow is milked, while in Europe and most other parts of the world where goats are milked, the job is done from behind, because goats have only two large teats, side by side, which are more available to both hands from the rear. We had found Nanny preferred the side position; for some reason she was very sensitive about people or dogs directly behind her.

Pat, having probably seen movies or photos of conventional goat-milking, tackled her from the rear. Drunk or sober, Nanny would not stand for it. She kicked him in the face. We four onlookers became so convulsed that we couldn't warn him before he tried a new tack: he straddled her, standing on tiptoe—she was a big goat—bent over, facing rearwards, until his face was lost in her twitching tail, and tried to reach under her with both arms. As soon as he was arranged in this clever, new, nonkickable position,

Nanny looked joyfully over her shoulder, sized up the situation, threw back her sharp, almost-straight horns, and nailed him in both buttocks at once.

Pat roared in agony and tried to dismount by hopping over her tail. He afterwards said he was sure it was his yell which startled her into her next strategy, but the rest of us knew Nanny had planned the whole thing. She backed up

rapidly as he hopped forward, thereby keeping pace with him, and she jabbed him at each hop. He tried to get off by throwing a leg over and falling sideways; each time she nailed him solidly, causing him to straighten up and holler again. She was very clever about the whole thing. She must have carried him twenty yards and twenty jabs before he collapsed and fell off, completely defeated.

The exertion seemed to have sobered Nanny up remarkably. After she had deposited her rider in an unhappy heap she trotted over to us in a straight line, looking rather proud; and when we ourselves had calmed down enough to milk her she was quite gentle. But her milk was a bit blinky, and we never let her near the beer crock again, although she whuffled and nosed around it often.

Every time our financial situation would begin to get dangerous, Pop would somehow manage to think up a new project to keep us going. But we never accumulated enough at one time to dig a well. We would save for a while, feeling very virtuous about it, then we'd count our assets, compare them with the staggering cost of the well, and go to Phoenix for a dinner and a movie at the Orpheum to forget our discouragement.

By the time we'd been on the desert for a year, the Robinsons had progressed well with their plans for a spa at their hot mineral well, one or two other families had started little truck farms, several homesteaders had left in discouragement, and a few were just sticking along like us. This annoyed Pop, who didn't care whether he was going up or down the ladder of success, so long as he was not static. Once he worked out a scheme which showed great promise: ironwood was fairly plentiful around our immediate vicinity, and the stuff was wonderful for cookstoves. So hard and dense it would sink in water, it burned like anthracite coal, with a slow, smokeless, and extremely hot flame. After all these months, Pop suddenly realized ironwood might have commercial possibilities.

He gathered a quantity, loaded the truck with it, and drove to Phoenix, returning in a very short time with an empty truck, a pocketful of folding money, and orders for as many more truckloads as he could haul. Furious at himself for not thinking of it sooner, he scoured the desert for more ironwood and sold several more loads. Then it became apparent that somebody had thought of it before him, and had gathered the stuff so diligently that once Pop had stripped our own place there was no more to be found.

Things started to look pretty bad again, and we began to think it might be wise to go back to New Mexico and take another fling at the apple business. But Pop swore he would not leave the desert without doing what he'd set out to do.

"I'm gonna grow citrus by God. Kitten, where's that ironwood money? I'm gonna take the truck to Phoenix."

He wasn't back that night or the next. About noon of the second day after Pop had gone, a homesteader who sometimes drove through our place on his way to the store stopped by with our mail, in which there was a most remarkable letter from the Veterans' Administration, addressed to my mother, condoling her on the recent death of her husband, who, it seemed, carried ten thousand dollars' worth of army life insurance, on which he had, according to the letter, wisely continued the premiums. The

letter requested a copy of Pop's death certificate, as a mere matter of form, and assured his widow that the ten grand would soon be rolling in.

My mother was stunned, and so was Sid. Obviously Pop had cracked up the truck on the way to Phoenix; the efficient Veterans' Administration, which kept close tab on all its charges, had already heard of it, and we were a headless family. I felt a sharp pang, myself, but I must admit that my sorrow was tempered somewhat by the thought that now we were going to have a well after all. I had only just begun to understand a little of life's materialism, and my emotions were all mixed up. Our ship had come in, but it seemed pretty sad in a way. I would miss Pop.

He drove up late in the afternoon, in a small sedan I'd never seen before. In the back seat was a cargo of what looked like sticks with burlap wads on their bottoms.

"What's everybody standing around looking so damn surprised about?" he asked. "Billy, you don't look so happy to see your old man huh what the hell's the matter with everybody? Is it the car? I didn't think any of you liked that old truck. I thought you'd be glad I traded it for a nice sedan."

We told him about the letter.

"That damn Veterans' Administration," he assured us, in words which have been repeated by countless millions since, "is the crummiest stupidest most cockeyed huh screwed up outfit in the whole government. I stopped paying my insurance the day the war ended and if those rock-headed scallywags have scared you all to death I'll go wring their infernal necks.

"Now look what I got," he said proudly, showing us the bundle of sticks in the back seat. "Young citrus. We're gonna set 'em out huh."

"What kind of citrus? How the heck should I know? They're citrus and I said we're gonna grow citrus."

Pop ignored our questions about how he was going to

water these thirsty youngsters for the four or five years until they bore their first fruit. There were a dozen plants. We carefully set them out in deep holes, with sticks tied to them so they'd grow straight, and we started them off with a whole barrel full of water, worth 45 cents.

It was the last water those trees saw, but they did grow a tiny bit, I'm sure, in the few days before they died. We never spoke of them again. Pop had gone to the desert to grow citrus; he had grown citrus; now he was ready to take us back home.

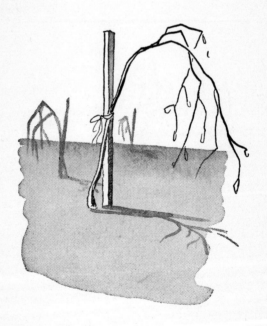

Part Three

IT WAS THOUGHTFUL OF POP TO GET A SEDAN for our long trip back to Mountain Park; his tastes usually ran to touring cars with tops that wouldn't work. Today a good automobile can make the same five-hundred-mile journey over the same road, now paved and well maintained, in ten or eleven hours, without endangering anybody's neck. But at that time there were long stretches of dirt road, detours, and numerous shaky bridges that collapsed every time there was a heavy rain. And tires, especially the kind we generally used, were constantly blowing out. Our trip out had taken three days.

All of us were collectors of odd items. Besides our regular household goods, there were piles of colored rocks we'd picked up from the desert, assorted firearms, dogs, furniture which had no intrinsic value but which we'd made ourselves and had become fond of, various choice items from Pop's junk pile, and so on. It would have taken a freight train to move all the stuff we wanted to take, and the sedan would hardly hold ourselves and our menagerie. Pop set to work building a trailer out of parts in his junk pile, Sid and I started sorting our own belongings, and my mother took off in the sedan to say goodbye to our friends and to pick up a load of groceries for the trip. We planned to make bivouacs along the way, for we were sure that no hotel or tourist camp would accept us with our dogs and our goat.

Three or four hours later a stranger drove up in his car, with my mother as a passenger. When she got out, we saw that she was shaky and disheveled, and was minus a shoe. We were pretty scared; it was obvious she'd had bad trouble. The man helped her into the house, Pop put her to bed, and then we learned that she'd turned the car over on the way home with the groceries. She liked to drive at a fast clip, and when she'd discovered that our "new" sedan was capable of going fifty miles an hour, she had opened the throttle along a slightly rutted stretch of road. One of the front wheels had hung in a crooked rut, the tire had blown, and the stranger, whose house was a half mile from the scene of the wreck, had heard the crash and had come running. He'd found her pinned half in and half out of the car, yelling like fury.

He'd thought at first she was all crushed and dying, then had discovered that while she'd somehow escaped serious hurt, the car's battery was dripping acid on her foot. She'd felt the drip, smelled the acid eating her leather shoe, and was scared, quite justifiably, that the damned stuff would chew her foot off before somebody got her out. The man had been unable to move her, and because of the position of the wreck could not remove the battery from under the floorboards. So he'd raced off in his own car to get help from other nearby homes (it was too far to come to our place), and for half an hour, until he returned, my mother had to lie under that car and feel the acid working through her shoe. It must have been a horrible feeling. When several sturdy men finally lifted an edge of the wreck and got her out, she discovered that she had no more shoe at all—it had been so badly corroded that it fell right off her foot.

It had been an ordeal, but my mother, as soon as she'd inspected her foot for the fifth or sixth time and made sure it was intact, rallied very quickly, and began to bemoan the fact that the accident would delay our return to Mountain Park. While Pop drove off to the wreck with the kind rescuer to see how much of a car we still owned, Sid and I pestered our mother over and over, making her tell exactly how it had happened. It was the first wreck our family had had, and it thrilled us.

We were somewhat surprised to see Pop pull up to the house only a couple of hours later in our own car, which was actually running under its own power. He and our benefactor (it pains me that I can't remember his name) had, with the aid of several jacks, rolled it back onto its wheels, changed the blown tire, straightened out two wrinkled fenders, rustled up a rather dilapidated battery somewhere, tinkered with the engine a while, and discovered that the car had lost little of its original enthusiasm for running. The frame was bent a fraction, perhaps; there was a decided shimmy to the front wheels; the body had a scar or two; and two windows needed to be replaced (they never were). But otherwise, the car was ready to go. Even the groceries were still in it, although they'd been scrambled a bit.

Next day Pop finished building the trailer, and we discovered that by leaving out the bulk of our colored-rock collection and most of the furniture, all our personal baggage and clothing and camping utensils would fit nicely into the contraption, leaving room in the car for ourselves, a few of our smaller treasures, and the dogs, which included our "Boston Terrier," his Scottish wife, and their four pups.

Nanny, who'd become a regular member of the family and was a milk goat only as a sideline, presented a problem. She had been spending all her nights curled up on the seat of the truck, and when the sedan replaced the truck, she took immediate possession, sleeping in it at night and hanging around it during the day, waiting for someone to open a door and let her in. The upholstered seats were an unheard-of luxury to her. She was an immaculate goat. (The superstition about all goats being smelly actually applies only to billy goats. One billy can make such an unpleasantness that, if he's traveling in a herd, he can cast a stigma upon them all. Nannies, as a rule, are very clean, and our Nanny was the purest of them all.) We'd have had no objection to letting her ride inside the car with us, but there just wasn't room.

The trailer would be no good for her: it lacked springs, and the combination of bumping and inhaling exhaust fumes would, we were sure, make her ill and unhappy and spoil her milk, besides hurting her delicate feelings. So we built a framework of slats along the right side of the car, bolting it to the fenders and wiring it to the doorpost and the hood, so that Nanny could ride on the running board. We put aboard a piece of canvas to cover her in case of rain.

We started early in the morning of the third day after my mother's wreck. None of us looked back at our tent-house. We had lived a good life there and we didn't want to get sentimental about it. The trailer bumped along noisily, its canvas cover making flapping sounds, the sedan purred more or less steadily, and Nanny actually seemed to enjoy her position on the running board. She got her sea-legs very quickly, and my mother would reach out from the front seat and scratch the goat's ears or pat her on the back from time to time to let her know we still loved her. And when Nanny discovered, going through Hassayampa, that she attracted a great deal of attention (people would glance idly at us, then spin around in a double-take, their eyes popping) she actually took to posing for her "public," sticking her nose out in the breeze and leaning forward as if to streamline herself.

Our trip would probably have been uneventful, except for the usual flat tires, had we not stopped for the night at Phoenix, not far from the sheep pasture where we'd bivouacked long before, on our way to the desert. There Pop got into a conversation with a fellow who told him about some sort of construction or engineering job going on in town. Since we were not returning to Mountain Park loaded with cash, perhaps that's what influenced Pop to go into town the next morning and investigate the job.

He came back to us with the disconcerting announcement that we were to proceed without him, and wait for him at my grandfather's house in La Luz, ten miles below Mountain Park. He said he intended to stay in Phoenix just long enough to make himself a roll of folding money, then he'd join us and we could all make our triumphant return to the farm together. We protested loudly, and my mother said she never wanted to touch a steering wheel again after her wreck, but we were treated to a long and successful harangue, and next morning we pulled out of our campsite, leaving him standing there waving to us.

Everything happened to us on that trip. Our delay in Phoenix allowed an eastbound rain storm to catch up with us, and by nightfall we'd had three flats. We carried four spares—one on the front bumper, one on the left running board, and two on the rear. Changing a tire on cars of that vintage involved dismantling practically the entire wheel, removing rims, unbolting countless rusty lugs, and struggling with a primitive jack. Without Sid's help my mother would never have been able to do it. The two of them would splash around in the mud, looking for tools, scraping their hands and bruising their fingers, while I walked Nanny and the dogs around, letting them attend to their natural urges and keeping them off the highway. Once a couple of friendly men stopped and helped with a tire, but during that day and the several days and countless flats that followed there were few passers-by, for the rain never stopped, and the roads got stickier and sloppier. I don't know why the rain seemed to cause so many flats; perhaps it washed up nails and sharp sticks which had long been buried deep in the dirt.

We made so little progress the first day that my mother

decided to drive all night. She had a lot of courage. We began letting Nanny ride in the back seat during the night, for with Pop gone there was more room in the car now, and it would have been cruel to leave her out on the run-

ning board in the wet darkness. The dogs slept on the floor as the car droned along, and Sid and I went on two-hour shifts, one riding in the front seat to keep our driver company and prevent her from dozing, while the other napped in the rear. We hung Nanny's canvas over the rear window which had lost its glass, and left the broken front window open for fresh air. The rain was falling straight down and not much came in.

By three o'clock in the morning we'd passed through the high mountains a hundred miles east of Phoenix. I was doing my stint in the front seat, and I remember our gas was quite low. We hadn't been able to find an open filling station in either Miami or Globe, the mining towns at the crest of the mountains. As we hit the winding road which led down to the rolling country of eastern Arizona, I betrayed my duty and dozed off. My mother was nodding over the wheel, dead-tired. She hadn't uttered a complaint all during the miserable day and night.

A loud and unhappy yell from Sid woke me about an hour later. The yell stirred up the whole contingent of passengers: Nanny bleated, the dogs yapped, and when I took a look through the windshield I added my own voice to the hubbub. We were driving straight at a body of murky, heaving water that looked as big as the Mississippi River, and was doubly terrifying in the yellowish light of our headlamps.

We stopped right at the edge of the water. It was so wide our lights didn't reach across, but they did illuminate several cars parked helter-skelter along the bank, with their drivers and passengers huddled in the rain talking to each other. A man who was standing beside a harnessed team walked over to our car and began giving my mother instructions for crossing. We were in the eastern foothills of the mountains, and the road ran across a small valley which had been flooded by the heavy rain. Fortunately, the floor of the valley was flat; the stream, although it looked huge and formidable and moved pretty fast, was quite shallow.

The man with the team was a local farmer who had come out in the middle of the night to encourage stranded travelers to get across while the flood was low, so they wouldn't be stuck on his property if the road later became impassable. The farmer told us that so far all the male drivers in the group had been afraid to try the crossing—"Maybe if a lady went first the rest of 'em would follow you."

"I know every foot of this road," he said, "and the water's still low enough so it won't drown out your motor. But just in case you do get stalled, remember I'm watching you and I'll come yank you out with the team."

Perhaps my mother wouldn't have tried it if she'd been feeling fresh, but by this time she was so dog-tired and anxious to get on with the trip that she'd have driven through a wall of fire had it been necessary. Without a word, she put the car into low gear and plunged in. Even though the stream's force was dissipated by its depth and breadth, it had enough push to make the car slew to one side, and my mother had to fight the wheel with all her strength. The trailer swiveled around until it was following us at almost a right angle, with its wheels dragging sideways. The water piled high on the side of the car, growling and splashing threateningly at us as we moved along. It was very muddy and evil looking.

Halfway across we ran out of gas. It was the last straw for my mother. After her long silence her simple and heartbroken "My God!" had the eloquence of fifty great oaths. We looked back to see if the farmer had noticed our plight and saw that he had been right about the other drivers becoming shamed into following a woman's example. They were churning behind us in a long line. When

we stopped the whole parade halted, for nobody wished to risk running off the roadbed into deep water by trying to pass us, and our trailer made it impossible for the car behind to push. Over the steady rumble of the water we could hear shouts and curses and screams, getting fainter and fainter as word was passed back along the line for the farmer to come up.

Very soon, he hove up beside us with the team, riding one of the horses. The water was making them stagger and they didn't seem to be liking it. Splashing about in the dimming yellow of our headlights (the battery which had replaced the wrecked one wasn't very good without the engine running to keep it charged), he hooked the team to our front bumper, climbed astraddle our hood with the reins in his hands, and pulled us on across. The stream had been about three hundred yards wide.

Safe on the east bank, we thanked the farmer, who asked us why we'd stopped. When we told him we'd run out of gas, he offered to hail one of the other cars, which were now chugging up the bank and splashing on their way, and ask for a few gallons.

"Why, if it wasn't for you, lady, the rest of them dummies would have sat there a week," he said.

She told him we had had enough of cars and gasoline and traveling to last for the time being, and thanks just the same. Whereupon she leaned back on the seat and fell asleep as if she'd been chloroformed. Dawn was beginning to break. Sid and I dozed off again; Nanny and the dogs were already sound asleep. The farmer went back into the stream to help another car that had stalled.

Very soon after sunup, Sid and I awoke together, feeling somewhat cramped, and saw that we had parked almost in the farmer's front yard. His team, still hitched, was standing by the house. We looked back at the stream we'd crossed. It still looked ugly, but daylight reduced it to its proper perspective, and we realized we'd seen much worse during the big desert flood of some months before. We were debating whether to awaken our mother, who was still leaning back against the seat, out cold, or whether to walk up the highway and look for a gas station or stop a car and borrow some fuel, when the farmhouse door opened and our good friend of the night before came toward us with a two-gallon gas can in his hand.

Sid and I thanked him graciously as we poured the gasoline into our tank, and we asked him, as we knew was proper, how much we owed him. He protested loudly that he was glad to do us a favor. The talking awakened our mother, who shook her head a few times, got her tired eyes into focus, opened her purse, and pressed a five-dollar bill into the farmer's hand, insisting that it was the least we could pay for the combination of towing and fuel. He absolutely refused pay for the towing, repeating that his motive had been to prevent a lot of marooned tourists piling up on his property, and finally agreed to let us pay for the gasoline. He was a very nice fellow.

We rolled on and on that day, stopping for only two flats. It still rained—the storm continued moving eastward and pacing us—and not once were we able to stop and make camp. We ate our meals from the stock of groceries in the car. Nanny was a good sport—she spent most of the day on the running board, with her canvas covering keeping her reasonably dry, and even the pups seemed to get into the spirit of things, adjusting their bowel schedules so that they all functioned together during stops. We made two hundred miles, stopping early in the night at Deming, New Mexico, a hundred-odd miles from our objective. We were fortunate enough to find a tourist camp which would admit us, after we promised to bunk the goat and the dogs in the car.

As the result of a night spent in horizontal sleep and a comforting wash-up and change of clothes, we were able to pull into La Luz that evening looking fairly presentable, if rather damp. We'd had but one flat during the last lap, and there were only a few blisters among us from operating the tire pump. My father's parents were very happy to see us, and, miraculously, the rain stopped almost as soon as we arrived, so we were able to catch our first sight of the sun in several days, just before it set. My mother ate a hot meal and vanished into the bedroom for a long sleep, and Sid and I sat up late telling desert stories to our grandfather, to his annoyance, for he preferred spinning his own yarns.

Next morning Pop joined us, not a bit richer than he had been. The job hadn't panned out, and he'd caught a ride all the way with a fellow who drove a big, fast car that plowed through the floods and the mud without a bit of trouble. Pop was terribly remorseful when he heard about our trip.

"I worried about you all the way," he said. "I figured sure I'd find you bogged down somewhere along the road."

It's a wonder he hadn't.

We rested for two days at La Luz. Sid and I renewed our acquaintance with Brown, the old colored man, while Pop walked around my grandfather's little orchard, admiring the trees and getting himself all worked up about the glories of fruit-growing, and my mother tried, rather unsuccessfully, to explain to her mother-in-law why the devil we'd gone out to the Arizona desert in the first place, when we already had such a nice farm at Mountain Park.

When we started up the long, steep drive into the Sacramentos, breathed the cool, thin air, and looked back over the panorama of plains and mountain ranges, and

thought of the pine forests and the rugged peaks above us, we wondered ourselves why we had ever left.

The people who'd occupied our farm had already evacuated when we drove rather quietly and modestly into Mountain Park, with our trailer and our goat and our dogs. The tenants had left some weeks before and had gone, curiously enough, to Arizona. (We heard from several sources that they planned to start a homestead out there.)

One look at the farm showed that we'd have to live elsewhere for a few weeks until we could fix the place up. The house was a mess, with the ceilings sagging and wallpaper hanging in strips, and the orchard had been almost completely taken over by brush.

My grandmother Bemis, whose house was on the hill overlooking our place, was delighted to see her peripatetic daughter again. George Bemis had died while we'd been on the desert, and the house seemed very lonely without him. She offered us accommodations until our own home should be fixed up. She had a great affection for Sid and me, and she had come to like my father in spite of herself, although she had always regarded him as something of a phenomenon, and she still stared at him sometimes as if unsure whether or not she should have locked her daughter in a closet when he first came courting.

As soon as we were settled temporarily in my grandmother's house Pop and my mother tackled the farm. The house was first on the agenda; Pop fixed the roof, repaired the floor, straightened the ceilings, cleaned up the yard—noting happily that most of his precious old junk pile was still out back—and then set out to clear the orchard. He was cheerful and optimistic, of course—the ruined place presented a staggering challenge and there were countless opportunities for his inventiveness and resourcefulness. I don't know what had happened to our old team of horses, but my grandfather in La Luz had a team he wasn't using at the moment; Pop brought them up to Mountain Park, devised a heavy brush-drag (it was nothing more than a sort of raft made of logs), hitched the team to it, and started pulling it through the orchard, smashing the huge growths of weeds and bushes.

My mother buzzed about the house, painting it, papering the most dilapidated walls, and working out ways to furnish it without the convenience of money. As an inventor she did well in her own right. Taking the back seat out of the car, she made a very nice living-room sofa, putting the cushions on two sturdy boxes and making a gay slip-cover to go over the whole thing, with ruffles reaching to the floor. Using this kind of ingenuity, fixing up the few pieces of furniture still left in the house, and brightening up everything, especially the kitchen, with pretty borders and trims and fancy curtains, she had the house livable within two weeks.

Sid and I, who were by then eleven and ten years old, respectively, were large enough to be recruited into the rehabilitation job. Sid was enthusiastic and useful; I regret to admit that my aversion to the endless chores of farming, which had become noticeable long before, was now even more pronounced. I guess I was the laziest kid in Mountain Park. I justified it to myself by thinking of stories I'd heard of men who became great and powerful because they were dreamers in their youth, and I set to work at trying to become a dreamer.

Accordingly, I sneaked away from chores at every opportunity, crept quietly into my grandmother's house, settled into a big easy chair she kept in a corner of the living room, and started reading. My ambition to become a

great dreamer was real enough, but unfortunately I lacked certain mental equipment for it. In earlier days I had read a great deal as an escape from teasings at the hands of my schoolmates. Now, in my grandmother's house, which had plenty of good books, I found that my tastes hadn't changed. Instead of reading fine literature and thinking of changing the world or building great bridges and cities, I pored over old copies of *Esquire*, which my Uncle Waldron, in El Paso, sent my grandmother regularly, and I mused about roulette wheels and wicked women and easy money.

I learned to creep into my grandmother's house so quietly and to blend into that chair so completely that often my unwitting hostess would walk through the room without seeing me.

Pop often suspected where I went for my gold-bricking, but since my grandmother seldom knew I was around, she was able to say truthfully, when he came crunching up her gravel driveway looking for me, that she hadn't seen hide nor hair of Billy. The camouflage was so good that once, when a gossipy crony of my grand-mother's came calling, I sat in that chair undetected for two hours while the two of them sat with their tea at the other end of the big room and talked about a girl near Cloudcroft who had had a particularly grown-up and fascinating operation. The caller told this story in great de-tail, over the shocked protests of my grandmother, who is a shy and gentle lady, while I listened, enthralled, and kept very quiet. *Esquire* seemed tame for weeks afterward.

Through everybody else's hard work, the farm was in more or less decent shape within a few weeks, and we moved into our own house. Unfortunately, it was too late to do much about a crop that year, so while Pop continued putting the finishing touches to the orchard and my

mother went visiting to renew some of our old friendships in the community, Sid and I started attending the
Mountain Park-High Rolls school again.

One would think our old buddies at school would have
been glad to see us back. Perhaps they were, but they
didn't show it. They knew where we'd been, all right.
Pop had had grandiose plans about Arizona and had aired
them about so much before we'd left that our homestead
venture had been discussed considerably by all the kids'
folks. When we'd returned meekly with nothing to show
for the expedition but a nanny goat that gave sweet milk
and a number of what we considered interesting stories,
the neighbors would not have been human had they not
passed a few caustic comments about us. Of course the
kids heard some of the talk, and it affected their feelings
toward Sid and me.

For a long time we were "desert rats" to the mob. We
retorted for a while by calling our taunters "mountain
goats," but since we had the only goat in those mountains
the phrase ricocheted back at us. We tried slugging the
matter out with our fists a few times; we'd grown healthy
and husky on the desert, but our opponents didn't seem
to have become stunted themselves in the mountain air,
and they were many to our two, so we generally lost. But
eventually we settled back into normalcy, just like in the
old days. Sid was a likable, easygoing kid who took a
teasing so well that it was no fun to rag him, and he picked
up his old friendships.

I was as belligerent and noisy as I had been, and I continued getting into fights, with Sid helping me sometimes

when I was outweighed or outnumbered, then whaling me himself when he got me home. Actually, the only difference between my social troubles before we'd left for Arizona and those I had when we got back was that for a while after our return Sid had been catching some of the ragging I always got, and so I'd had a welcome, if temporary, companionship in my woes.

Some of the fights at home between Sid and me were classics. No holds were barred. Because of the difference in our sizes, I had to use wiles. His favorite trick was to pin me on my back, spread-eagle, and blow in my face— a thing I couldn't tolerate. During the fist-throwing phases of our battles I'd try to work in close so my shorter arms could get a fair whack at him, and he'd try to hold me off.

Once I managed to get a good flying-mare hold on him and throw him: a heating stove, red hot, with the letters "LIBERTY" raised on its cast-iron surface, happened to be in the way. For several years he carried the reversed letters "YTR" and part of the "E" branded on his left buttock; so far as I know he still wears them. Another time he threw me out of a bedroom window without bothering to open the sash. A ditch ran past the house, right under the window; I landed in the water amid a shower of glass, picked the shards out of my skin, and went back into the house covered with my own blood and intending to spill some of his to match it. I carried a handful of rocks for the purpose. I honestly think Sid was scared of me when he saw me coming with those rocks. My Pop had heard the ruckus and stopped the fight before further mayhem was committed.

Shortly after our return to the Mountain Park school I talked myself into a brawl with a large, well-conditioned boy we'll call Egbert, who lived on a farm above ours. Egbert loved to fight, and he knew boxing, which was my misfortune, for I belonged to the roll-in-the-dirt school of rough and tumble, while Egbert used his large fists scientifically. He was demonstrating this admirably on the way home from school one afternoon. I forget what started it, but that's not important. Like many kids that age, when I was mad enough to fight I cried, which made me even madder, for I knew my tears were mistaken for something else. I was flailing and bawling like a bull calf at this Egbert fellow, and getting well pounded, when Sid broke in and tried to take Egbert over. In a very short time he'd whipped the both of us.

The day after the fight I was at bat in a baseball game in the schoolyard. Egbert was behind me, catching for the opposition. Came a very low pitch and Egbert, certain I wasn't interested in a sure "ball," ducked under my bat to catch it and heave it to second, toward which my predecessor at bat was edging from first. At about the same time, I decided I wanted the ball—it was low but it was slow, and I let fly, catching Egbert on the base of the skull with an awful thud and stretching him out at full length. He got up unsteadily and came for me with his eyes watering and slightly out of focus, but fierce. Waving the bat feebly in front of me, I protested that it was an accident (it was) and that the place for a catcher is *behind* the batter, but he was sure I'd tried to kill him. He'd have

· 198 ·

slaughtered me on the spot had the teacher not come to herd us back to class.

After school Egbert was waiting for me, and he waited every day thereafter for some time. I began to be a little the worse for wear. One day he informed me, after the regular session had ended and I was wiping the debris from my visage, that he had to go home in a hurry the next day, and so wouldn't be able to give me his attention. He was apologetic about it, but assured me he'd worked out an alternative. He was going to lay for me in the morning *on the way* to school. I had a hard time sleeping that night. I thought of everything, including murder. I'd brought my .22 rifle with the bent barrel back from the desert, and I had a few cartridges. But while I was young enough to think of such a thing, I was old enough to realize that society might not approve.

There was only one other way out: not to go to school. I couldn't tell my folks about it; my mother was inclined to be overprotective, as we'd found to our embarrassment before—she'd have stormed over to Egbert's parents and then I'd never have heard the end of it. My Pop would have insisted on giving me boxing lessons, and since I was having to learn fighting the hard way anyhow, I didn't want to be bothered. So I took my lunch and my books and holed up in Frog's Mouth, a huge boulder shaped exactly like a frog emitting a croak, which stood on a hill overlooking our farm, the school, and the road between. It was a favorite hangout of mine. You could bask in the sun on top of the Frog, or sit cozily under the edge for shade or protection against rain, and you could observe all approaches for enemies. I often used it for goldbricking when I didn't sneak up the hill to my grandmother's house, and would sometimes watch my Pop searching all over the place for me.

It was a pleasant morning. I sat among the rocks and spotted Egbert as he came swaggering along, peered around for me on the road, stopped and watched my house for me to emerge, then shook his head in anger or disappointment, and continued to school, still looking around for me. At noon I built a campfire under the side of the Frog, ate my lunch in small bits, and read my schoolbooks with real enjoyment, probably learning more than I would have in a week's time in the classroom.

In the afternoon I watched Egbert come jogging along in a hurry, headed for home. Then the stream of other kids came by. When the parade had passed I went home innocently and entered the kitchen door just in time to hear my infernal brother ask our parents "Why wasn't Billy at school?" When I cussed him out later he said he'd asked out of sincere worry and that I should have briefed him sooner. I told him he ought to have had sense enough to guess what had happened. I got a whale of a walloping out of that with Pop's number-one belt, the one he saved for our more serious felonies. I suspect he laid it on more because I'd ducked my enemy than because I'd ducked school.

My Pop was not a ready man with the rod, and I don't recall ever having had my britches fanned without cause, but he did believe in making a whipping last when it had to be administered. His system was to make the culprit receive the whipping standing in a doorway, with both hands on the jamb, so there would be no instinctive jerking around of the hands to protect the seat. (It is to his credit that he respected a sense of dignity; he never made

us drop our pants, but he'd frisk us for protective padding.) Sid was a perfectly normal whooper when he took a licking; his voice would rise and fall like that of a tortured banshee. For some reason, I only cried when I was mad, not when I was hurt. It was not bravery; something in my brainbox simply worked backwards, that's all. But when I received this particular licking, I noticed Sid watching with admiration while I flinched under the belt but kept my face composed, and suddenly I too began to think it was bravery.

I'd read something in a book about how the Spartan boys were trained to take punishment, and was very impressed with the one who let a fox gnaw his innards under his shirt, without an outcry. So when I heard Sid describing my latest whipping to a group of his buddies on the way to school next day and saw them look at me with, for the first time, something approaching admiration, I felt great. Even Egbert seemed slightly awed.

Caught in my own foolishness, I stated loudly to several boys at school that no pain could get an outcry from me; on the way home that afternoon I invited anybody present to bust me over the head with his books. One sturdy lad bent an inch-and-a-half thick Reader, with stiff covers, into a U over my sconce; my knees buckled slightly and the jar made my eyes water, but it really didn't hurt much (to my amazement). It was very spectacular. Everybody took his turn, they all went home with bent books, and my fame spread rapidly. Next morning I had a new trick for them. I had tried, privately, switching myself on the forearm with a willow shoot. It hadn't hurt much, so I openly invited all comers to whack my arms with sticks and small tree branches. That hurt like the devil, but I stuck it through, resolving to do more careful research in the future.

Still highly impressed with myself, I had an idea which I hoped would set me up for all time as the most intrepid lad in Otero County. Our house was on a hill; the post office-store was on another, in plain sight, about half a mile away, across a pretty little valley. The local creek had cut a gorge down the middle of the valley, and the road to the store crossed the creek over an old wooden bridge, which

was supported by heavy log underpinnings. The planks of the bridge were two-by-tens, and long ago a two-foot chunk had been broken out of one plank, near the center of the bridge.

I found that by climbing under the structure, standing on one of the log braces, and stretching hard, I could get my head up through the hole. It would be a spectacular, a supreme, a magnificent feat, to let a car go over my head.

And it wouldn't really be dangerous, either, for nobody but local people used the bridge; they all knew about the hole and always took pains to straddle it, for even the best auto tires of that time would blow in such a hole. But my stunt would take some nerve, just the same, for an auto hurtling at one's head can be an awfully fearsome sight, even if you're sure he'll miss. I decided I'd better put myself to the test before doing any advertising.

So, late in the afternoon of my third day as a Spartan, I stood on the log under the bridge, listening to the creek gurgle below, and feeling the breeze flirting in my hair and blowing small bits of dirt from the planks into my ears. I was musing happily on the name I'd made for myself and which I was about to enhance, when I heard a car coming down the hill from somewhere above our place. There was a straight, steep stretch of two hundred yards as the road ran along a cut in the hill where our house stood, then a sharp bend, and another straight stretch, very steep, which bore down on the bridge. It was a loosely graveled road, quite bumpy and rocky. I saw the car was coming down the long stretch pretty fast. It was a high old sedan. I thought, "This fool better slow down or he won't make the bend," but he didn't slow down and he did make the bend, and he came hurtling at me. I saw he would straddle me and suddenly I felt very cool and confident about the whole thing. I knew I would pass the test, getting, at worst, a little grease in my hair, for it looked like the kind of old car that dripped. I was that observant of detail, I was so calm.

But I hadn't counted on the fact that the car might be

driven by someone who could be rather upset by the sight
of an apparently disembodied head sitting on the bridge
and leering at him with the wind blowing its hair. The
sedan had two-wheel brakes; the driver made the most of
them on that loosely graveled, steep stretch, with ten
yards to go. I ducked just in time. He hit the bridge sort

of sideways. As I dropped to the creek bed and started
running I heard one end of him crash into the guard rail,
while a front wheel thudded into the hole where I'd been.
As I scuttled around a bend and started up the bank, I
heard him stop with a hollow rattle on the far side of the
bridge.

I got up the hill to our house, moving at a fast crouch

through the brush and shaking considerably. There was a fearful ten minutes during which I sat with a book in the living room, looking as innocent as I could, and waited for the man. I was sure he'd follow my tracks down the creek bed, up the bank, and home. But he didn't come, and after many more minutes I finally worked up the nerve to peer out the window at the bridge.

My victim was down there with his car, bolting a fearfully bent wheel on his spare tire rack, having already mounted the spare. As I watched he walked around the car, looked sadly at the mangled rear fender which had struck the railing, and then he went over to the edge of the bridge, got down on his hands and knees, and leaned so far and peered under so long that I was afraid he'd fall in. He had the air of a man who'd looked under there several times in the past quarter hour, knowing he'd find nothing, but hoping for some clue which would tell him he wasn't crazy. After a bit, he shook his head unhappily and drove away, with a sharp list to port which could only mean a broken spring.

I had never seen him before, and obviously he didn't know to whom that God-awful head belonged. Perhaps he was never sure he saw a head at all, for otherwise he'd have told the story around the community and I'd have heard about it. I felt badly about the whole thing, for I knew nobody in that area could afford the luxury of blown tires and bent wheels and broken springs.

However, word of my other Spartan activities had got to some grownups in the community, and I think several of them considered this as final proof that Sidney and

Katrina Mauldin had spawned a nut for a younger son. Several days after the bridge episode I was walking past the postoffice-store, in front of which was a much-whittled bench where local men often sat and whiled away their days when they had nothing else to do. One of the bench's most steady patrons was a man who had a little cattle ranch in a canyon five miles down the mountain, and as I passed him I heard him say to the storekeeper:

"If that wuz my kid I'd drown 'im."

This infuriated me so much that for several nights thereafter I lay half awake dreaming of the fellow going under for the third time in one of the deeper pools the creek made along its tumbling course down Box Canyon: him gasping and choking and me standing beside the pool laughing.

Motor transportation had become as much a necessity to our community as horses had been to our forefathers. All the farm-owners had trucks of one kind or another. There were few really big trucks, for most of the fruit was sold by the ton to independent haulers, who would drive their huge rigs right to the farms, load up, and haul the apples to distant places (where the fruit passed through the hands of so many dealers and middlemen that the big, fancy eating apples we sold for a cent or two a pound cost a nickel apiece on grocery counters).

Some families used their utility trucks for passenger purposes, loading the kids in the back for a Saturday trip to the movies or a dance at Alamogordo, eighteen miles down the mountain, but every year a few more found they could afford a regular passenger car. With all this rolling stock around it was natural that all the kids learned to drive at a tender age. I got my first lesson, shortly after we returned from Arizona, in my grandfather's 1925 Dodge, and within a very short time I was allowed to solo. My mother, who gave me most of my lessons, was a good instructor despite the fact that she had hated to drive since the Arizona wreck and the harrowing trip which followed it.

Sid, I think, was born knowing how to drive. He was a natural with machines. Very soon after we'd settled back on the farm, Sid and I got a simultaneous urge to own a car of our own. By pooling all my personal belongings, including an ancient Oliver typewriter, with a few of his own, and talking persuasively, Sid traded a Model T Ford away from a boy named Albro McPherson. Somehow, my brother got the thing started and drove it home under its own power. It was a very early Model T, and it had only an engine, a chassis, and four tireless wheels.

Although the car was legally half mine, Sid pretty well took it over. He was a shrewd fellow, and this deal of ours was typical of many that followed. He had traded all my stuff, and a fraction of his own, for the car. The ownership of the machine was equally disproportionate, but in exact reverse. However, my brother could be charming at times like this; he was a fine backslapper, and somehow I never really felt cheated.

By dint of scouring the countryside, just as Pop had

done long before for sprayer parts, Sid found equipment for the flivver. A tire here, a horn there, a magneto coil another place—it all added up. Pretty soon the Model T not only ran well, but it looked fine. We made it into a nine-passenger car by laying three planks across the frame. So that no one could say we were driving an unsafe vehicle, we wired the boards to the frame to prevent their sliding around. One advantage to the rig was that when the car had trouble getting in motion (the friction bands, which propelled all Model-T's, were badly worn on this one), the passengers could push by simply slipping down between the boards and running—this gave the car the appearance of a centipede with four wheels—until the thing became self-propelled, at which point the pushers would leap back into their seats, leaving their legs dangling should another shove be needed. Sometimes feet were needed for brakes, too. Of course we knew better than to apply our foot brakes at a speed in excess of ten miles an hour. The friction would have been terrible.

In this machine, with passengers numbering from two to nine, we helled all over the countryside, making several trips to Cloudcroft, where the road was steep, twisting, rough, and narrow, and where, in several places, there was an almost sheer drop of a thousand feet. Although a number of tourists, and an occasional local man who had partaken too freely of Cloudcroft's hospitality, have been killed on that Cloudcroft road over the years, it's interesting to note that none of the Mountain Park kids ever went over the side while learning to drive. We were a little reckless at times, like all youngsters, but we knew what we were doing. Anybody who learned to drive on those roads could drive anywhere.

However, it was a wreck which finished our Model T. One afternoon we were bowling to High Rolls under a full head of steam (25 m.p.h.), with some important mission in mind, and with an almost-full complement of passengers, when we encountered a farm hand driving a big

Holstein bull up the side of the road. It is a well-known fact among people who drive in rural districts that bovines can be depended upon to stand safely aside until it's too late for a fast car to stop, and then saunter across the road.

This particular bull eyed our flimsy vehicle, tossed his head, and stepped into the middle of the road fifty or sixty yards in front of us. We knew the brakes were no good, but none of us wanted to break an ankle by dragging feet at that speed. So we froze fearfully on our seats and hoped for a miracle, such as a sudden head wind, to slow us down. Air resistance, plus the tiny bit of brake band remaining in the old relic, got us down to perhaps 20 m.p.h. before we piled into the bull, but the force was enough to knock the animal off his feet, hurl one front-seat passenger completely over him, and pile the rest of us up on the hood and against the dash, both of which collapsed under the strain. It was a fine tangle of kids. None of us suffered wounds worse than bruises, but the Model T had perished: its radiator had been molded around the front of the engine, and both front wheels had splayed out sideways.

Our enemy, although scratched and somewhat dazed, was obviously the winner. The bull's escort looked us over calmly, then without a word prodded the creature to its feet and continued driving him up the road. After we had unscrambled ourselves, we all went home, got the family car, and towed the Ford's remains to Pop's junk pile, where it became just one more item in the mountain of "spare parts."

Sid later went on to bigger and better cars, trading them all around, fixing up 1927 wrecks, trading them for 1928 wrecks, fixing those and swapping for 1929 models, and so on, through Chevrolets, Fords, Austins, Plymouths, and God knows what. I never owned another auto until I grew up.

But I still liked cars. Whenever a friend or a relative showed up in something new, I'd beg shamelessly to drive it, and if refused, I'd sit in it and pretend. My favorite pretending auto was an elegant red Marmon touring car which had somehow found its way to our automotive graveyard. It had no wheels and no top, and hadn't run for years, but all the rest of it was there. It was very racy and had some of the lines of a motorboat and some of an airplane. Since, at various times, I had ambitions to be a flier, a boater, and a racer, the Marmon served many needs. On airplane days the gearshift lever was a joystick, and, wearing a pair of toy goggles, I would lean menacingly out of the cockpit, jiggling the stick and squeezing the knob when troops were within strafing range. And I dreamed up the PT boat long before the Navy thought of it, sitting in that Marmon on rainy days.

My airplane passion reached a climax the day an enterprising aviator in a red biplane flew low over our house, scaring everybody to death—air currents are bad in those mountains and we expected this fellow to pile up in one of our apple trees. He had hardly roared out of sight when I raided Pop's pile of lumber and tools and started manufacturing a "Spad" fighter plane based on a picture in one of those "Ace Aviator" pulps popular between the last two wars. This was no toy I worked on; it was a full-sized plane, twenty feet long. I made the fuselage cross-sections out of two-by-fours, diminishing them in size so that there would be a proper taper toward the tail, then built a framework of ribs out of laths, intending to cover them with fabric, although I wasn't sure where the fabric would come from.

I was pretty well along on this framework when Pop found it behind his shed. He blew his top. The laths, which had been bought for repairs on the house, had been expensive, and I'd used every one of them. But he was a wise and tolerant Pop and after the initial explosion he gritted his teeth and watched while the monstrosity grew day by day. At the end of a week, I had a wingless, tailless, engineless fuselage, covered with burlap feed bags I'd ripped open and tacked on, in lieu of regular airplane fabric and out of consideration for our household sheets.

The cockpit was very elegant; it had an instrument panel made of a board whittled to fit in the proper position and several instruments I'd liberated from various wrecks, including the Marmon which had been equipped with a real, honest-to-gosh altimeter. I'd painstakingly cut holes in the panel to fit each instrument and, besides the altimeter, had installed three speedometers, an ammeter, and a couple of gas gauges. A bit of broomstick was attached to the floor by impaling it on a big nail I'd driven up through the bottom. Although the nail was sufficiently flexible to give the stick freedom of motion, it provided enough resistance for me to feel a real "drag" as I wobbled the stick.

An old sofa pillow made a fine seat, and one of Pop's discarded leather belts served admirably as a safety belt around my belly.

As soon as the cockpit was finished I couldn't wait to sit in it and strafe troops. After flying a few missions, I intended to scout around for more laths and burlap and make the wings (my design had strayed from the "Spad"—a biplane—and was now to be a monoplane) and tail, then put the craft on wheels instead of the apple-boxes on which it now rested. I knew an engine was out of the question, but I actually had the half-formed notion that it might possibly sail a little way through the air if I could talk Sid into pulling it fast enough with a tow rope attached to the car, someday when the folks weren't around. It was a pretty flyable-looking fuselage.

However, when I got into that authentic-looking cockpit I found that I didn't miss the wings, and since my enemies were always before my guns, I never looked back and didn't notice the lack of a tail. The "wheels" were underneath and out of sight. The propeller was theoretically spinning and invisible anyway. My plane sat on top of the hill near the shed and the house, and I found that when I was in the cockpit no ground appeared immediately ahead and there was an actual sensation of being in the air. I could get an illusion of fast movement by lining up an edge of the cockpit with a tree or a hill, then moving my head slowly, making the landscape slide along.

I really intended to do more work on the plane, but I had so much fun just sitting there and flying around that I kept putting it off and soon would have forgotten all about the rest of it. Then my Pop had his round. He'd been keeping an eye on me, thinking of those laths and musing about a kid who could work like a demon on something like that and then goldbrick on an easy chore.

On my second day of playing in the cockpit, Pop walked up several thousand feet of thin air, paced along at 175 m.p.h. until he caught up with me (I was cruising at half throttle, lining up a convoy of Red Cross trucks which I knew contained ammunition), leaned a friendly arm on the cockpit, jiggling it and making me shoot way to one side of the convoy, and interrupted my dream by commenting loudly,

"Pretty ratty looking airplane."

I rose to the bait and asked him what was wrong with it; I showed him my fine instruments, the throttle which had been the spark control on the Marmon's steering wheel, and all the rest of my work.

"It can't fly," he said. "Look—no wings, no tail, no wheels, no tailskid, no ailerons, no lots of things, including no engine."

I protested that my plane was authentic enough while I was in the cockpit, but he went on criticizing, saying he was ashamed to have a half-finished airplane in his yard— it was worse than having no airplane at all. For two weeks he made me spend all my time after school and on weekends searching for materials, and he didn't let me stop until there *were* wings and a tail, and if you've never tried to build full-size wings on a full-size fuselage, with frail laths and no knowledge of how to make them stay on, don't try. Pop wouldn't let me cheat and prop the wings from beneath, either.

"Did you ever see a plane with wings that had to be propped up?" he asked.

I finally finished that part of the job with baling wire and rope strung from the cockpit to the ends of the flimsy wings, and with a tail assembly that had to pass an inspection as rough as the Civil Aeronautics Authority has ever devised.

But even then Pop didn't let me alone. "What about a motor?" he asked.

An engine was out of the question; the framework wouldn't hold any propelling device heavier than a rubber band. Pop finally relented on that part, but he made me put little wagon wheels underneath and a piece of bent iron at the rear for a tailskid. The finished product looked like the pride of the Pandemonium Air Force after surviving a hail of flak and with its engine out for a 6,000,000-hour tuneup, and I was so sick of the sight of it that I was overjoyed when a stiff wind smashed it up against the side of the shed and I was detailed to break it up for kindling wood.

If I'd been a good kid around the place, doing my work on schedule and trying to make myself helpful, I think Pop wouldn't have begrudged me the use of his laths and the fun I had. But I was a goldbrick, and I was all too prone to start huge experiments and projects, then tire of them and leave them half finished. Pop was wise enough to know where that sort of tendency led; from then on, though he was more than liberal about letting me start things, he always saw that I finished them.

Somehow, Nanny got pregnant shortly after we returned to Mountain Park from the desert. So far as we knew, there wasn't another goat within fifty miles, and how she managed to get in a family way will always be a mystery. Nanny had her children in due course (two billies and a nanny), and from then on she seemed intent on populating Mountain Park with goats. Evidently inbreeding doesn't bother the creatures, for the most shameful kind of incest went on among our goats, to such an extent that eventually Nanny gave birth to a pair of daughters that had been sired by one of their mother's great-grand-sons. As near as I can tell, that meant her daughters were their father's great-great-aunts and their own great-great-great-aunts.

With all those goats eating our pasturage, we thought for a while of going into the dairy business in a big way, to make them pay their own keep. Several of Nanny's daughters shared their mother's talent for producing sweet milk, and after awhile we had a small but steady clientele among the dozen or so summer people who owned bits of property between Mountain Park and the resort town of Cloudcroft and who came up for their health. Their doc-tors had advised them, in many cases, to drink goat milk, and they were delighted to find ours was so tasty.

We never got enough profits from our goats, however, to make it worth while keeping them. The intelligent thing would have been to kill the billies, except for one or two good specimens for stud purposes, and to concentrate on the nannies. But all Nanny's kids were lovable charac-ters and we just didn't have the heart to be scientific. One of the billies helped solve this problem by bumping him-self off. He had inherited a liking for acrid-tasting objects from his soap-eating mother. He found an old paper sack blown into some bushes, and for two or three weeks he nibbled occasionally at it, making it last a long time. But one day he overindulged, eating the whole bottom of the sack at one sitting, and it wasn't until after he suddenly dropped dead that we investigated the sack and found it had contained arsenic, a spraying ingredient, and had evidently been left lying in the open by one of the tenants who'd occupied the place.

Nanny herself had a rather spectacular, if untimely, end. When it was all over we felt she'd have preferred it that way, for sad as it was, she wasn't getting any younger and she was the kind of character who would wish to go out with her boots on, so to speak, rather than with hardened arteries. Nanny had become addicted more and more to wandering about the countryside, and we were afraid a car might run her down, so we started tethering her to trees and posts. One day we tied her to a tall tree near the apple-house, a largish building on the side of a hill, where we stored unsold fruit. A lot of succulent alfalfa grew around the building, and next to soap and beer Nanny liked alfalfa best.

Since ropes were no good on Nanny—she liked to chew on them—we used a light steel chain, fifty feet long, attaching it to her horns with a bit of soft copper wire so that the chain wouldn't chafe her. Just after dark of the day we tied her to the tree at the apple-house, a sudden thunderstorm came up. Before anybody could get to Nanny and lead her to shelter, lightning struck her tree, the current traveled through the chain and the wire, and Nanny went out in a blaze of glory, a veritable incandescent goat. It didn't burn her or mess her up at all; she was beautiful and serene in death.

We were pretty broken up about Nanny's death, and within a short time we bought a cow and got rid of all our

goats except one, an infant billy who'd taken a shine to me
and who used to follow me around like a little pup. I
argued my folks into letting him stay because he was very
intelligent and liked to learn tricks, and I had a vague notion that there might be some future in owning a circus

goat. I had discovered his talents one day when I'd been
walking through the orchard, had bent over to tie a shoe-
lace, and felt four hard little feet land in the middle of
my back. The little cuss had jumped up there all by himself, and when I tried walking along all bent over, he kept
his balance and stayed there. I taught him to jump on my

back when I leaned over and said "Allez-oop!" and then he learned to scramble up on my shoulder when I straightened, and he'd balance up there with his feet bunched, swaying and looking like a parrot as I walked along. Of course, he'd do it whether I said "Allez-oop!" or not; I was always careful to say it *before* he could jump up— that way it made him look trained.

Inevitably, I got into head-butting contests with him while he was little and had soft, button horns. We used to put on a fine show, with him jumping all over me and me challenging him to butting contests. There's no telling how far we might have gone as a team if he hadn't grown up rapidly. His horns got sharp and so did his feet, and I couldn't take it any more.

But I didn't miss him for long. After the goats had gone we'd bought a milk cow. With her came a fine bull calf, and it was given to me with the standard old proviso: "You've got to take care of him or you can't keep him." He was a Jersey, and while Jerseys don't grow very big, they're smart and tough. Like a fool, I started training this calf like I'd trained the goat. I didn't want him jumping on my back, of course, but I did butt heads with him. His head was even softer than the goat's had been, and sometimes I knocked him right on his tail, after taking a good run at him. But this was *his* natural-born game, not mine. He took it like a sport, studied my techniques, and got better every day, so that after about a month he could fight me to a draw every time.

He grew fast, and shortly he was turned out on the hillside pasture, where I visited him often at first. After a

while, however, I was going to school again and thinking about other things, and so he grew to be a year-
ling without much contact with me. Until one day, thinking about anything but Jersey bulls, I was walking through

a flat field with my eyes on the ground and almost bumped
into him. The pasture was supposed to be fenced from the
field, but he'd got through somehow. He eyed me in
a friendly fashion, and I said hello to him. He sure
looked big. He must have weighed twelve times what I
did. And he had a pair of very mean little horns. With a big
playful grin on his face, he dropped his head and charged me.

I remembered very quickly—your mind works fast at
times like that—about how bulls are supposed to shut their
eyes when they charge. As I was jumping out of his way,
I hoped this baby knew he was supposed to do that. It
was a long way to the nearest fence. Sure enough he
missed, but in a twinkling he wheeled and came at me
again. He meant no harm; this was our game, and I'd
taught him. By hopping and sidestepping and running I

worked my way to the fence and rolled under it, in a terrible sweat. He seemed very hurt about my behavior; after staring at me for a moment, he turned his back and walked stiffly away. We sold him shortly thereafter and I didn't miss him.

We'd given away all the pups we'd brought back from the desert, except one, named Big Boy, who'd become my dog. He had inherited his father's coal-black coat. As he'd grown up he'd become a real bum. He ran away every night and chased over the countryside with dogs way out of his league. They were bigger, faster, tougher, and smarter. But nobody was as brave as Big Boy. He was always picking fights, and he never picked one with a dog smaller than he, or even the same size. They had to be three or four times bigger or he wouldn't touch them. This wasn't gallantry; it was just that he thought he was a big shot.

He fought like a cat, getting under an opponent and worrying its abdomen. He never won a fight in his life. After all night binges he used to drag himself home in the mornings with ghastly wounds. Once a big mutt actually gutted him with one slash of his teeth, and we had to push some of Big Boy's insides back where they belonged, after brushing the dirt and leaves off, and sew him up. I picked up all the details of that particular fight from an eyewitness. Seems the big dog had been strolling with an equally large mutt of a girl friend, and Big Boy had decided he wanted the girl. Bristling, he had walked up between the

couple and given the girl his attention. She'd sneered at him, moved off to a safe distance, and sat down to watch the fun. If she hadn't sneered and hurt Big Boy's feelings, he might have put up a better fight. As it was, she'd sort of taken the heart out of him.

Another time, he made the mistake of tackling a huge German police dog. I'd been walking to the post office with him, and this kraut had come out of the bushes and started across the road, minding his own business. Before I could grab Big Boy he was under the kraut, working on his belly. The police dog very efficiently kicked him out from under, grabbed him by the throat, and started killing my dog with such coolness he looked almost bored. I jumped on the enemy and started trying to wrestle him off Big Boy. This got him sore and he turned on me. I don't blame the police dog for it, really. After all, he had just been crossing the road peaceably and had been attacked for no reason.

After he'd chewed on me a while, the kraut's manners got the best of him and he went on into the bushes on the other side of the road. Big Boy didn't seem a bit abashed, even though I wore a bandage for some days and showed it to him at every opportunity.

One night he went out carousing and didn't come back. After two days I began to feel bad; on the third day I was very unhappy, for I did love the pooch. At supper I started snuffling around, and Pop went out to check on where Big Boy had last been seen alive. He came back shortly to tell me that a little black mutt answering Big Boy's description had been flattened three days before by a fast automobile going through High Rolls, a mile away. I snuffled even worse, and finally Pop couldn't stand the noise, so he took a shovel and went to High Rolls to bury Big Boy. Somebody showed him where the carcass had been thrown into the bushes, but it wasn't there any more. It must have got fragrant and somebody else had buried it.

Pop comforted me, told me Big Boy had been bound to get his eventually, considering the riotous life he'd been leading, and that he'd get me another Big Boy. Pop gave me all the standard arguments that are given kids whose dogs have croaked. For a week I went around unhappy, but each day it got better.

One morning about ten days after the Big Boy tragedy, I was given the chore of hitching the team to the log-drag and flattening some weeds in the lower part of the orchard. It was a fine, sunny morning, and I discovered that not only had most of the pangs of sorrow disappeared, but that I was actually speculating on what kind of dog to get next.

So I was riding along on the drag, whistling tuneless songs and enjoying the fact that the contraption felt like a raft floating on gentle swells, as it bobbed over clumps of weeds, when something black and smelly and mangy hurtled out of a clump of brush and leaped on the raft, almost bowling me over. It was Big Boy. His hide was torn, and caked with dried blood, and one of his paws looked as if it had been chewed almost off. He yapped and fawned all over me.

I hated the sight of him. Here I'd gone through a week's misery on his behalf, suffering and bleeding inside for him, then finally, by dint of great will power and strength of character, had dried my tears and determined to build a new life for myself. And here he was back again. No dog is worth two wakes, I decided, especially a worthless cur like this one. Damned if I was going to go through all that unhappiness again when he really conked off. From then on Big Boy, although he once again took his place in the household, could come and go as he pleased. I made a point of not caring. I don't think he ever noticed the difference in my attitude. He kept on fighting and raising whoopee every night until he finally disappeared for good.

My grandfather's team, which we borrowed for so long that he learned to do without and decided to let us keep them, consisted of an eighteen-year-old dun mare named Duchess and a twenty-year-old white horse named Bud. That's getting along in years for working horses, but they were very big and sturdy, and the kind of work we had for them was not likely to wear them out. Bud was a wise old beast who must have done time in the service as an artillery horse. He knew all the army tricks of malingering. Since Bud knew how to let Duchess do most of the straining, it was fortunate that she was a high-spirited zealot who loved to pull things.

When the woodpile got low, Sid and I sometimes hitched the team to a sledge with steel runners, which Pop had built for the purpose, and went bumping off into the hills after firewood. The sledge was more fun to ride than the regular wagon, and it could go places where wheels would bog down or break. I never tried to get out of this particular chore. Not only was it adventuresome to drive the team through the woods and play at being a pioneer and Conestoga wagon driver, but it gave me unlimited opportunities to smoke cigarettes with impunity.

We always spent the better part of a day on this job, and when we had got a load and started home in the evening, it was a sight to watch Bud loaf and throw all the work on Duchess, who accepted it eagerly. It was especially noticeable going up hills. Bud would puff and blow and heave, and then hold his breath until veins stood out all over him and it looked like he was about to bust a gusset, but when you looked at his traces, they were slack, while Duchess' were so taut you could play a tune on them. To the uninitiated, Bud appeared to be doing everything. Sometimes he would even forge ahead of his harness-mate as much as three feet, which looked very convincing, although it actually threw even more of the weight on her.

Bud was such a smart old duck that when he was used for light plowing he didn't need a bridle. He knew how far to go, when to turn, how widely spaced furrows should be, and everything else. Plowing was his art, and since the ground was pretty soft, Bud preferred to be a prima donna and do it alone. The only time he was ever hitched with Duchess on a plowing job he deliberately fouled the lines and then led the poor mare right over a buried stump, causing her to almost rupture herself when the plow hung up.

Duchess and Bud both loved to be ridden, and for old horses they had a lot of zing. Of course it would have been foolish to let them accelerate over a slow trot, except for occasional gallops for short distances; they might well have dropped dead from overexertion. But a nice thing about them was that they never reminded you of their age: they were always chomping and tugging at the reins and acting as though they would just die of sorrow if you didn't let them make like a Western movie, so you never had the feeling that your steed was an ancient work horse.

They were both so gentle that I often rode one or the other of them bareback and without a bridle, guiding them by tugging on their manes, or just by leaning heavily in the direction I wanted to go. Duchess and I developed a circus trick which I think she enjoyed even more than I did: her huge, round body swayed easily and steadily when she was in a slow gallop, so I learned to balance on her back, first on my knees and then on my feet, standing erect and with no handholds, while she loped across a little, flat field, doing maybe twelve or thirteen m.p.h. It felt like we were

doing sixty, with the wind in my ears, and although it was easy as pie, it was probably very spectacular to watch.

With all this horse stuff, it was inevitable that I should go through a cowboy phase. Sid was never bitten by that bug, since he was going in heavily for mechanics, already having become a competent automobile doctor at the age of twelve. Several of the boys I knew in the community had pretty good riding equipment and horses, and two or three of them actually did part-time work on the numerous ranches around Cloudcroft and down on the foothills and plains. They were the aristocrats among us because the proceeds from this work enabled them to get hand-tooled saddles decorated with fancy leather stirrup covers, called tapaderos, the points of which were so long that they almost dragged the ground, and with an abundance of silver-plated conchos. They had silver-mounted bridles and Justin boots and Stetson hats and leather chaps, all properly buffed and scarred by either hard riding through rough country or by assiduous scratching done at home with the point of a rusty nail—the object was to look like a working cowpuncher, not a guitar player from Holly-wood.

Even the boys who, like myself, were farmers' sons during the week and only did their riding on holidays, were able to get together fairly authentic outfits and reasonably good saddle horses. When Cloudcroft had its big annual summer rodeo, all the Mountain Park-High Rolls sons of toil were able to clatter up the mountain in a posse and cause the tourists, who watched the rodeo from shiny cars, to think that the whole countryside consisted of ranches and that there wasn't such a plebeian thing as a farm within fifty miles.

Then I would come along and screw up the works. Having plodded up the steep five- or six-mile mountain trail to Cloudcroft on Duchess or Bud, I would galumph into the rodeo grounds astride the only saddle in our family, a high-backed, wide-seated, long-skirted, bare-stirruped, single-cinched relic my grandfather had used in the 70's. It was an honorable, respectable, but horribly obsolete saddle alongside the modern, low-cantled, tapaderoed, streamlined, Spanish-horned jobs with swells so broad and seats so small that they looked as if a man had been poured into them.

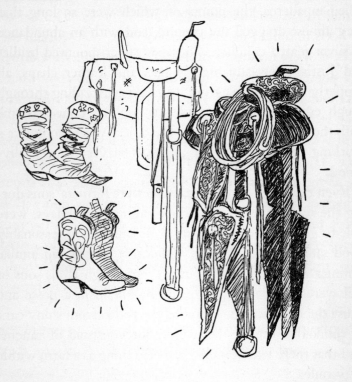

The popular headgear at the time was a cream-colored or black hat with a moderately wide brim and the crown mashed in and molded like a cake pan. My top-piece was a secondhand Boy Scout hat. It wasn't too bad, since the top would mash in the approved manner, but I had to give the brim its proper, racy curve by soaking the hat in a solution of sugar and water and then holding the curves in position while they stiffened and dried. Every time it rained, or even when the air was moist, the sugar would soften and the brim would flop disconsolately.

For footgear, I took a pair of English riding boots my mother had worn out long ago, nailed chunks of leather to the heels to build them up Western style, and worked the backs of these makeshift heels into the correct slant down to a point at the base. Since low tops on cowboy boots were coming into vogue, I cut my mother's boots down to eight inches, curving them at the tops, and embellished them with an assortment of hearts, spades, diamonds, and clubs. Happily, my feet at that age were about the same size as my mother's, except for length. There was about an inch of free play in the tips beyond my toes, and within a very few days after I started wearing the boots the toes curled up, Persian fashion, and nothing I could do would make them stay in line. But it would have been unthinkable to come to the rodeo with clodhopperish farmer shoes.

Starting for the rodeo at the same time as the rest of the mob, I'd turn up an hour after them. By that time they would have pulled up in a cluster alongside the grandstand and mingled with a group of young and old authentic cowpunchers who were watching the proceedings from the backs of their horses or were perched on railings with their hats on the backs of their heads. There, they were under the admiring eyes of throngs of tourists who sat in a long glittering row of cars strung out along the far side of the arena.

When I'd arrive among the horsemen, those who did not know me would look me over with indulgent and somewhat humorous eyes, while those who did have the honor of my acquaintance would look the other way and edge off, obviously afraid that I, patently a rube from an apple farm, might speak to them and so identify myself with them.

So, involuntarily aloof from other riders, I would sit for a while on whichever of our noble steeds I had chosen for the occasion (it was usually Duchess—she was better formed; and Bud had several old harness scars in conspicuous places) and watch the fun. The Cloudcroft rodeo was generally good, featuring mostly local talent and emphasizing practical skills such as calf roping, but with plenty of spectacular things like trick riding.

Along about the wild-cow-milking contests, halfway through the affair, I'd notice that other horsemen in the audience had dismounted, out of consideration for their ponies, and I was always in a new dilemma at that point. If I stayed aboard my horse, not only would I be conspicuous—and I desired to be as inconspicuous as possible —but also it would look as though I were rough on my steed. But if I dismounted, I'd have to tie my horse's reins to something. Now, one of the most elementary bits of training for a good pony is for him to learn to stand fast when his reins are on the ground. When the others dismounted, they dropped their reins, with studied carelessness, in front of their horses, and while a horse may mooch around for bits of grass, he may not move out of his little radius and drag his reins. If something startles him he can jump around a bit, but he may not go far, else his master will be ashamed.

Neither Duchess nor Bud knew this trick. They were practical beasts, and they figured that if somebody wanted them to stay put, he should tie them up. Otherwise, they were wont to wander about and graze, stopping only when they stepped on a rein (unforgivable) and could go no further until they lifted the huge and offending hoof. I knew either of them would just as soon stray right into the arena if I let them go.

So I would dismount and hold the reins, hoping nobody would notice, but of course everybody did. The rodeos always lasted several days, and I'd stubbornly show up at each one, until I finally came to hate Duchess and Bud, blaming everything on them. I've often since felt ashamed when I've remembered that. Duchess was a lady and Bud was a real he-man of the old school, and either of them had more damn spunk and character than any prancing, frippery, jug-headed little broomtail around. Any fool can learn to stand still when his reins are on the ground; not every horse can be wise and tolerant and patient with a kid who ropes a scrub tree with an old piece of manila, ties it to the saddle horn, and expects the horse to yank it up by the roots and pretend it's a wild steer.

But I was a kid, and even though I knew I couldn't hope to obtain, even by working, enough capital for fancy rigging, I did want a "real" horse the worst way. So when I was twelve, in the eighth and last year of grade school, my folks promised me a good riding horse if I would study hard and be valedictorian. I applied myself to the task and actually managed to triumph over a graduating class of six or seven competitors. Stuck for a speech, I got my mother to ghost-write one for me; it lasted two minutes and was something stirring about "Perseverance Wins." It had one gesture in the middle—a sweeping of the arm over the head and a pointing toward the sky—and my mother promised to sit in the front row at the school auditorium and signal me by putting her hand to her face when it came time to make the gesture.

On the big day there was an audience of fifty or sixty. I was so jittery I made the two-minute speech last one minute, hardly stopping for breath. I forgot to watch for the signal, ending up by making the gesture when I'd finished speaking, as a sort of victory salute.

I got my prize a few days later. She was a little sorrel mare who had been owned by several people and was sold to my folks for eight bucks by a fellow from La Luz Canyon; he threw in her young colt for free. Two things were wrong with the mare: she hadn't been saddle-broken properly and she was terribly neurotic. You could get a saddle on her and climb aboard all right, but from then on anything was likely to happen. I learned later that one of her former owners had beaten her half to death with a stick of stovewood after she had shied at something in the road and had thrown him. Since she was basically high-strung anyway, and since the beating had been administered mostly on her head, this treatment had probably scrambled her brains hopelessly.

The little mare had a powerful maternal feeling for her young son, seeming determined to protect him from a world she considered full of dangers and mean humans. Since no amount of drumming on her ribs with my heels would make her go a step past our main gate once I had shut it between us and the colt, he accompanied us everywhere, skipping around in the funny, long-legged, irresponsible manner peculiar to colts, with his mother swiveling her head around from time to time to make sure he was all right.

On one of our very first rides we passed a big, fenced-in field where dwelt a huge black mule. I didn't know mules had a very special and peculiar hatred for colts, or I wouldn't have gone that way. This big fellow saw us, roared at us, cleared the high, barbed-wire fence with a mighty bound, and went after the youngster, chasing him back down the road toward the house. The mare, who was about half the mule's size, wheeled so fast she almost spilled me. She took off in pursuit, her ears laid back in fury. I was pretty scared.

I don't know what would have happened if the terrified colt hadn't been fast on his feet. He went bounding down the road with the mule almost on top of him and us clattering along behind the mule. I couldn't stop the mare; I couldn't even turn her. We went a good half mile before the colt seemed to get a new spurt of energy and increased his lead by so much that the mule gave up and turned off a little trail to one side. My ferocious lady faltered a second as she came to the turn off, and I was afraid she was going to continue the chase; but her primary interest was her colt. After she caught up with him she nuzzled him for a while, and then seemed to remember for the first time that she was carrying a rider. We went home.

The mare had a horror of automobiles. Every time she saw one, even if it was standing still, she would leap to her baby and cower between him and the car, shivering violently. When an approaching car honked she would explode in terror, rearing and bucking and snorting. Bridles and neck-reining meant nothing to her when she was excited. Even if I pulled on one rein, as though she were a work horse or I were an Eastern jockey, until her head was right in my lap, it made no difference to her. Pieces of paper in the road, particularly if they moved or fluttered in the wind, gave her the fantods.

In short, she was the shyingest horse alive, and nothing would cure her. I considered fitting her bridle with one of those atrocious Spanish "spade bits," which have sharp edges that painfully lacerate and pinch and humble the strongest-mouthed horse. But then it seemed to me that any horse that required such drastic treatment would be better off sold for dog-meat.

My steed had a very shaggy coat; when she'd been in brushy parts of our pasture I always searched her for cockleburs before saddling her. One morning I missed a bur that had buried itself deep behind her forelegs, where the saddle cinch girded her. I cinched her up tight, hopped aboard, and started happily down our drive toward the gate, with Junior tanglefooting behind us in his erratic way. The gate was on the side of the slope fifty yards below our house, but the road from house to gate, designed for cars, was almost a quarter mile long. It consisted of a long, straight, gentle climb from the gate to a hairpin turn, then another straight stretch right to the house.

The lower half of the drive was cut into the side of the hill; the upper half ran along the ridge, with a steep drop on either side. I liked to gallop my mare along this drive. She ran nicely and I didn't have to worry about her blowing a gasket like Duchess or Bud. This time, she went into her run willingly enough, but about halfway between the house and the hairpin turn, the bur dug her and our route became vertical. That girl could buck. She went up high and came down with her legs stiff, her four feet bunched. At each landing my backbone telescoped until my chin was in my lap.

While the mare confined her pitching to the road I stayed aboard all right, suffering only from shock and from fear that my neck was broken—my head was bobbing like a lollipop on a snapped stick. But when she started bucking down the steep hill at the side of the road, the situation got critical.

That damned old saddle became worse than no saddle at all. From front to back my tail was perhaps eight or ten inches thick; the flat saddle seat was a good eighteen inches long, which gave me plenty of sliding room, and what with the leather being old and stiff and cracked, there was a lot of friction. If I'd had a match in my pocket it would have set me afire. Up on the road my seat had been more or less horizontal, but now every time we landed there was enough forward slant to throw me off balance and toward the mare's ears.

I lost my right stirrup on about the fifth hop down the hill; on each succeeding jump it flew up unerringly and smacked me in the teeth. Realizing that my time up there in the air had about expired and that I was due to greet the earth any second, I tried to free my left foot, then became panicky when I realized my boot had passed almost completely through the stirrup and was stuck. The thought of being dragged was awful; I brought the foot up and struggled with it with my left hand, holding the saddle horn with my right. This maneuver threw me so completely off balance that the next impact heaved me bodily over the saddle horn and deposited me on the back of the mare's head. Happily, my foot came loose at the same time.

At the same instant I caught a fast glimpse of that infernal colt. He was bucking joyfully right alongside us, in a perfect imitation of his mother.

The sudden weight of my body on the mare's head stopped her. Straddling her neck, with my head out between her ears, my fanny in the air, and my arms wrapped tightly and desperately about her jaw, I remained there for a moment while she shivered and blew through her nose. Then I slid off, landing in a disgraceful heap under her nose. There's a horseman's code that says you've got to get right back on again, but I had lost the greatest part of my cowpunching ambition during the past minute. I was not interested in codes applying to professions from which I'd resigned. With both legs peeled on the inside surfaces, my face pulpy from the beating the loose stirrup had administered, my back in a shambles and my tail tattered, my head aching, my teeth loose, and my eyeballs hanging from their sockets, I led the mare home, unsaddled her, and shooed her off to pasture, with the colt still bucking along beside her.

Actually, any horse is justified in exploding when jabbed by a cocklebur, but in view of this one's generally bad behavior I didn't feel very forgiving. Although I did ride the mare several more times before I gave up "cowboying"

completely, I suffered no pangs when I finally sold her, and I gave the new owner a complete bill of particulars about her eccentricities, warning him that whatever he paid me would be too much.

Although I lost most of my interest in horsemanship, I still wanted a pair of real cowboy boots very badly. They were a sort of mark of distinction among the kids around that part of the country. A truly fashionable young man of the day went to town wearing a white shirt with the sleeves rolled high and tight almost to the shoulder and with the top two buttons undone, exposing some chest. A wide belt was buckled tightly about the waist of a pair of well-creased trousers (never slacks), one leg of which was tucked, with careful carelessness, half in and half out of the top of a fairly conservative but highly polished cowboy boot. This tucking was very important. Only one leg could be tucked. The other pants leg had to come demurely down and cover the boot top. The idea was to look as if the wearer didn't really want to show off his boots—one of his pants legs had just accidentally hung up, that's all.

There were some slight variations. The more dudish fellows, and those who had biceps too small to display, turned their shirt sleeves up neatly halfway between wrist and elbow. And the lady-killers among us wore torquoise-and-silver bracelets. These bracelets were supposed to be trophies of conquests; a man never wore a bracelet unless he'd got it from a girl in town, and he was supposed to have got it only as the result of having tricked, persuaded, or overcome the girl into favoring him with her intimate embraces. Judging from the number of mountain boys who wore Alamogordo girls' bracelets, you'd have thought there wasn't a virgin in the lot after the age of ten.

I had neither boots nor bracelet; I had only a single white shirt, a single pair of nice trousers, and a belt. With

a whole summer ahead of me after graduation from grade school, I set about finding ways to raise the twelve or fifteen dollars necessary for a pair of boots. For a while I tried becoming the Crowell Publishing Company's representative in Mountain Park, having been attracted by an ad for ambitious young men. I trudged through the hills with a canvas sack full of current copies of *Collier's*, *American*, and *Woman's Home Companion*. The deal was that I was to keep some ten or fifteen per cent of the cash sales and mail the rest back to the company, along with the top half of the covers of unsold magazines. There wasn't much of a market for Crowell around there, I discovered; after a week of hard labor, I sold three *Collier's* and one *Woman's Home Companion*.

For a while I toyed with the idea of cheating Crowell. They had the naïve idea that once you'd cut off the top half of a magazine cover, it was so mutilated that nobody'd want it. Actually, who misses the name of the publication and part of the full-page ad on the inside cover? Nothing could be simpler than to mail the required half covers back to the company, then sell the slightly marred magazines at half price and keep all the proceeds. I still think I was a sucker not to do it.

I answered another ad and tried peddling Cloverine Salve for a while. The stuff came in flat, round, tin boxes, and allegedly was good for cuts, burns, and abrasions. The company sent me a supply of Cloverine and a catalogue of the prizes I'd get after selling a dozen, two dozen, or more tins. I felt let down when I saw the catalogue because I'd gathered from their ad that "ambitious young men" would make good cash money. I reread the ad and found I'd misunderstood it, but it dawned on me that the radios and watches and other prizes would all have cash value, and once I'd won them I could sell them.

So I set out over the same route I'd followed with my magazines, knocking on every door in Mountain Park and High Rolls, covering a good ten miles a day. Finding the salve market rather better than the magazine market, I sold six tins. I suspected it was because of the "premium" I'd been authorized to give away with each tin. The premiums, which I carried along in a big roll under my arm, were huge and garish color reproductions of religious subjects, a copy of the Ten Commandments with blue and pink doves flying about the border, and various sentimental paintings of dogs and family scenes, the kind often found on feed-store calendars. These works of art were printed on heavy, glossy paper, "suitable for framing."

Six tins of Cloverine weren't enough to get me any kind of prize, let alone a radio or watch. I tried, in desperation, going back over the route and offering two or three pictures with each can, but I got rid of only one more. I wrote the Cloverine people and asked what they wanted me to do with the remaining two or three dozen tins, but I never heard from them. I suppose it was unthinkable to them that anyone carrying their product could fail to sell it all. Eventually I gave it all away; Cloverine will be happy to hear that nobody ever refused a free can of their salve.

Still early in the summer, I accidentally took a fling at the bootlegging industry. In company with a youth I mistakenly thought was my friend (he shall remain unidentified), I was walking through a stretch of woods not far from the Mountain Park post office-store when we saw a woman and two men in a little clearing, discussing something with gestures and loud voices. We stepped behind some trees and moved closer to see what they were up to. The woman, whom we recognized as the leading High

Rolls whisky manufacturer (she was proprietor, distiller, cashier, and advertising manager—in a word, the whole enterprise), had a gallon jug of amber fluid in her hand. The two men, whom we recognized as her leading buyers and consumers, were talking animatedly with her. We couldn't hear the words, but we saw money and the jug change hands. There was more talk, then one of the men scooped up some leaves and soft earth, and the other lovingly laid the gallon to rest and covered it.

When they had gone, we disinterred the jug, took it to the shed behind our house, and there found eight pint bottles, into which we poured the moonshine. Five of the bottles had corks; the other three we stopped up with wadded paper. Each of us took a bottle under his jacket and we set forth to find customers. There were plenty of prospects. The first man we tried was the school bus driver, who hauled kids of high school age to Alamogordo. He was thirsty, all right, and he had the required quarter, which was the ridiculously low price we'd decided to charge for the sake of a quick turnover, but he was understandably hesitant about buying whisky from bootleggers who were not even minors, but decidedly subminors.

Knowing this man's terrible thirst, we decided that his refusal was a strong indication that, if we kept on, we would run into prospects even more reluctant, and sooner or later word would drift around that kids were peddling hooch. There was no telling where it might all end.

So we buried the eight bottles (they undoubtedly needed aging anyhow) and decided to wait until we grew older or somebody grew thirstier before selling it. Our acts, both in stealing the whisky and in trying to bootleg, had made us more or less members of the underworld. Within a week after we buried the booze my partner not only violated the normal code of young boys, but he committed the most unforgivable crime possible in the underworld: he ratted. He shot off his mouth all over the place, and furthermore he must have put all the blame on me.

I will skip over the embarrassing details of how a delegation consisting of the lady distiller, her two customers, and several grim fellows (who must have expected to help drink the gallon, otherwise I can't see why they were so interested) came calling, and under their eyes and those of my father, I dug up the eight bottles, poured their contents back into the jug, and handed it over. The men carried their jug away, the lady bootlegger gave my Pop some specific advice on the handling of children, and she left, too.

The next day I passed a softball game in the little park behind the store post-office. All the kids stopped playing and hollered their opinions of a thief low enough to swipe whisky belonging to poor men who couldn't afford the loss. One of the loudest hollerers was my accomplice of the week before. I learned a valuable lesson in morality from that: if you're going to do something nefarious, do it alone.

I decided to go into legitimate business, and tried setting out cabbage plants at fifteen cents an hour. It's backbreaking work: you take a big bunch of the tiny plants in one hand, and with a T-shaped tool which has a bayonetlike blade, you punch holes in wet furrows, slip the plants in, and push the mud over the roots. After ten hours of almost continuous stooping and aching and sweating in the sun, you've got a dollar and a half. But there's a satisfaction in looking over a big field studded with greenery you've put there yourself, and fifteen cents an hour wasn't bad at all for a kid my age. I did that for three days and made four-fifty, but then there weren't any more fields to set out. That's the trouble with that kind of job: to make it steady you'd have to pull up all the plants and start over, which wouldn't satisfy your employer.

Early fruit started coming in—cherries, plums, and a kind of ugly little apple with a yellow-green skin which people who know apples recognize as a delightful thing to eat, but which suckers in grocery stores pass up for big, fancy, pulpy, juiceless, expensive, red ones. I took a basket of assorted fruits from our place and, using two apple crates as a sort of open-air counter, set up shop at the side of the road near the bend at the store post-office, where cars had to slow down on the way to Cloudcroft, planning to catch me some tourist trade. I set my wares out attractively in those little wooden berry boxes you find on store fruit counters, each box containing a quarter or a half pound.

Business was slow, and I had to keep wiping off the fruit every time a car came by and threw dust all over my establishment. My first customer was one of those char-acters known to all country people: a cigar-smoking huck-ster in a Buick, wearing a sweaty and bulgy summer suit, who obviously took great pride—having come, according to his license plate, from El Paso, a city of a hundred-odd thousand—in his ability to outsharp "natives."

This seedy bourgeois haggled me out of practically my entire stock, worth two dollars at my prices, for fifty cents. Actually, he bluffed me. When I didn't seem swayed by his arguments, he picked up all the boxes he could stack on his pudgy arms.

"Ya can't tell me this wormy stuff is worth more than four-bits," he said. Then he slid a half dollar at me and drove away in his Buick. Oddly enough, the coin rang true when I tested it.

I went home, picked more stock out of the orchard, and had hardly got back to my shop and opened for business again, when a gigantic logging truck, hauling fifty-foot pines down from Cloudcroft, came grumbling around the bend in the road. A man riding on the running board of the truck's cab yelled a warning at me just in time for me to jump before the end of one long log swept around the curve. It smashed my entire business into bankruptcy.

The summer began to look pretty grim.

My mother's brother, George Bemis, had taken up residence in El Paso with his family, and they all came up to Mountain Park for part of each summer. The grownups would stay at my grandmother's house, and the kids, George and Bob, who were about Sid's and my age, would horse around the countryside with us. We had four other cousins who generally spent time with us during the hot season. There was Jane Schumacher, a dignified girl several years our senior, the daughter of my mother's sister and her mining-executive husband. They were also from El Paso. It was Jane's dress I'd worn at the disgraceful Tom Thumb Wedding.

The Schumachers, who drove a big black seven-passenger Lincoln, spent all their time with my grandmother and we saw little of Jane, which was all right because she was a girl. We only missed her because she was just learning to smoke and had plenty of real tailor-made Philip Morris cigarettes.

There were Dick and Steve Loomis, the sons of our Uncle Guy and my mother's eldest sister Polly, from Las Cruces, New Mexico. They had a sister, Betty, who, like Jane, wasn't with us boys much. My main recollection of Betty was of having several violent arguments with her about such things as sex. She was four years older than I. Her mother felt the girl should be sheltered. Betty believed babies came by way of storks. I had lived among goats and knew better, and I didn't hesitate to give Betty the benefit of my knowledge, without the delicate embroidery and technical terms one learns to use with girls as one grows older. When I told Betty how her presence in this life came about she threw rocks at me and said nobody could talk that way about her folks.

This particular summer all the cousins came at once, and our house and my grandmother's were filled to capacity, which was lucky since I had a new idea for a commercial venture and needed help. I got Bob Bemis and Steve Loomis interested. Behind an old shack at the lower end of our place, which was sometimes occupied by transient fruit pickers, was a very ancient privy, a two-holer, which was badly in need of paint and fumigation, but was otherwise in good shape. Keeping our plans secret and waiting until a day when nobody was around, we wrestled the privy onto the sledge, hitched up the team, and hauled the thing a mile up the Cloudcroft road, unloading it at a pleasant spot where the road widened and was shaded by two huge cottonwood trees.

Working very fast, we took the door off the privy, cut it in half, and nailed it back on again—sideways, so that it covered the bottom half of the doorway. Knocking a plank out of one side so we could squeeze in and out, we set to work with the boards left over from the door and built a counter, a few shelves, and a cover for the toilet seats, which we had decided were singularly unattractive for our purpose. We were making a soft-drink stand. The weather was getting hotter all the time; it was a long, stifling drive from the plains to Cloudcroft, and we figured tourists might like to have a cool drink on the way.

The privy had reeked of the odor peculiar to old, abandoned outdoor johns, but we found that sitting in the open air away from its pit had sweetened it considerably within a few hours. There was really nothing wrong with it. We took the fifty cents I'd made earlier from selling fruit and bought some sugar and an assortment of flavors of Kool-Ade, a powder you mix with sugar and water. From home we borrowed pitchers and glasses and spoons. Right behind our "Drive-in Soda Fountain" was a convenient fast-running irrigation ditch full of crystal-clear, ice-cold mountain water.

We'd have liked to doll up the privy more, but there was no paint, so we were limited to scraping some of the rust streaks and stains from the surface of the planks and covering the shelves and counter with clean white paper. It looked pretty neat. We had located so strategically that whole lines of cars could park in the shade while their passengers drank, without disrupting traffic at all.

Finishing late in the afternoon of the day after we'd started, we decided to set up shop in the hour or two remaining before sunset, just as a test. Ten or twelve cars went by, but they didn't seem to see us, let alone stop. So we realized that advertising was essential. We spent the evening making signs with water colors on big sheets of paper and pasting the paper on boards. One sign said:

DRIVE IN
*
SOFT DRINKS
*
COOL AND REFRESHING
*
500 YDS

The next said the same thing, "400 YARDS," the next "300," and so on.

Next morning early we set up the signs, nailing them to fenceposts, first pacing off the distances so the signs would be accurate. Then Bob and I climbed into the booth with a bucket of ditch water and the rest of our stock, hoping the first customer wouldn't require change because we had none.

My brother Sid had joined the enterprise with great enthusiasm and had helped us put up the signs. As Bob and I sat in the booth, our hopes high, Sid and Steve Loomis stationed themselves outside to help direct the cars to good parking spaces, to serve customers who wished to remain in their vehicles, and to bring supplies of fresh water when needed. It was still too early for much traffic, and so the four of us made ourselves occasional Kool-Ades and wondered what a good secondhand cash register would cost. We thought of setting up a whole chain of stands throughout southern New Mexico.

By noon we had gone through a package of Lime powder and were halfway through a package of Cherry; each package made about half a gallon. At least thirty cars had passed, most of them tourists. We weren't fools enough to think our building attractive. We realized that there are prettier things than privies, and we knew it needed a coat of paint. But we hadn't thought it would disgust people.

An occasional car would actually slow down at our first sign (the slowing cars always contained a fat, perspiring wife; a scrawny, perspiring husband-driver; and a backseatful of kids with their tongues hanging out). Invariably, as the car drew abreast of us and we tried to look very alert and businesslike in our clean shirts, the lady would open her mouth in horror, turn quickly to

her husband, who never even glanced at us, and all the kids would watch us out the back window, with their little mouths forming O's, like a bunch of monkeys, as the car disappeared. People like that would patronize filthy restaurants where the glasses were never washed and the kitchens crawled with cockroaches, but the sight of a clean drink-stand made of a respectable old toilet repelled them. There is no accounting for tastes.

We stuck it out for three days without a single customer, until we'd drunk all our Kool-Ade, then abandoned the stand, taking the glasses and spoons home. The privy disappeared within a week—obviously somebody needed it for its original purpose or for a tool shed and appreciated its qualities.

As the summer went on, all the cousins went home, and I still needed dough for a pair of boots. The Cadwalladers, a family who owned a thriving orchard that produced very fine and succulent sweet cherries, had built themselves a large and handsome fruit stand near the store-post office, having had the same idea as mine about selling to tourists, but on a bigger scale. They were eminently successful, doing a weekly gross business of hundreds of dollars, with long lines of cars waiting to buy a quarter or half dollar's worth of cherries to eat on the way to Cloud-croft. Some of them would buy whole crates. I knew it would be foolish to apply for a job as store manager at the height of the cherry season, so I took a job picking the fruit for the Cadwalladers at a cent and a half a pound—plus all I could eat when nobody was looking—and bided my time.

Sure enough, when the boom ended they started to close up shop, for the fruit stand's daily take became too small to justify an adult spending all his time behind the counter. I offered to keep the stand open, selling their leftover fruit at a percentage.

They agreed to this, so I lined the stand with white paper, using merchandising techniques I'd learned from my two recent bankruptcies, set out the fruit in attractive displays on the counter, and for the first time that summer found myself making money. The streams of tourists had thinned to a trickle and there wasn't much fruit to offer, it being late for cherries and early for apples, so I didn't get rich, but I made enough for a ten-dollar pair of boots, which I bought promptly and wore for two years afterward. By the time the boots finally and luckily wore out, a doctor had to operate to remove two of the worst ingrown toenails he said he'd ever seen. I spent two weeks on my back with my feet in the air before they'd healed enough for me to stand on them.

In the early fall of 1934, when Sid and I were both supposed to start riding the school bus eighteen miles down the mountain to the Alamogordo High School, we managed to get sick. Sid developed a spot on his lung which put him in bed for three months and I got acute appendicitis and then developed kidney trouble as a result of lying around in bed after the operation. For some weeks, therefore, my brother and I spent our time in a horizontal position on the sleeping porch of our house at Mountain Park.

We were both too bedridden to fight with each other, so we spent our time playing games and reading. Sid engrossed himself with *Popular Mechanics* magazine and discovered new ways to dissect a watch. He also managed to acquire, through dickering with friends who came to visit and talk with him through the sleeping-porch screen, an ancient battery radio and a pair of earphones.

Some friends in El Paso sent us a pile of books, including a six-volume set of Ernest Thompson Seton's woodcraft books. These delighted me, and I wondered why I had ignored for so long the natural beauties of our countryside. Since it looked as though there would be very little school to worry about until at least half the winter had passed, I determined to learn everything I could from the books while in bed, and then put my knowledge to practice when I was able to get around.

As soon as I was allowed outside I built a wigwam in the back yard, following Seton's directions carefully. I used young willows for the framework, covering them with assorted bits of old blanket, carpeting, and canvas, all rudely stitched together. It was hardly weatherproof, but it was very colorful and actually authentic-looking. After all, didn't Indians use paint to achieve the same patchwork effect? I made flaps at the top, the idea being that by arranging the flaps to work with the wind, the fire inside the wigwam would draw nicely and not smoke up the interior. It really worked pretty well; I could build a fire inside and stay for thirty minutes at a time before I was driven out by fumes.

I continued my studies of Seton inside the wigwam during most of the daylight hours, feeling sorry for Sid at first, for from his sickbed on the porch he could see the fun I was having. But he told me Indian stuff didn't interest him at all—he'd found his life's work in radio. He had actually got the old set working and spent all his time with an earphone clamped over his head.

Before Seton entered my life, I used to hate nights on that sleeping porch. The wind made lonesome, moaning sounds in the high pines over in the pasture, crickets chirped mournfully, and coyotes gossiped on far-off hills. I had always felt myself cut out for city life, and one of my worst horrors was of dying and being buried in those mountains, so lonesome and dark and sad at night. But now I began to enjoy the nights, and think of the happy woods-creatures crawling around in the brush eating each other and trying to keep from being eaten. I got bitten hard with the romance of it all.

As soon as I was able to roam a little away from the yard I took to the hills and played at being a pioneer and trapper in the great Northwest. Within stone's throw of the house, and so close to the road that I could hear people talking and horns honking, I'd be creeping through the brush, "blazing" a trail with a knife so I wouldn't get "lost."

Sections in the hills above Mountain Park were bountiful hunting country. Deer was the principal game, but there were occasional bear hunts in some of the mountains. While deer preferred the higher, wilder country, many often moved right into our pasture when gunners started swarming through their homeland during hunting season. The deer would get to liking the easier winter forage in the pasture and every year half a dozen or more would settle down there permanently.

Deer cease to be pretty denizens of the wood when they move in on a farm. They become varmints, especially if you have tender apple trees for them to gnaw or a garden of late vegetables for them to raid. While it was against the law to knock them off out of season, or at any time without a license, there was a sort of understanding between local residents and the forest ranger, who lived at High Rolls and doubled as the game warden. So long as nobody slaughtered deer just for the fun of it, there was nothing wrong with taking a little free meat which had been fattened by one's own vegetables and apple-tree bark, and my Pop sometimes went out and got us a deer.

I remember once, when we still had our goats, the ranger and his wife came to play an evening's bridge with my folks. Like everybody else, he used our back door and, on his way to the kitchen, passed through a little corner room where we kept butter and milk, stored meat, and sometimes did our laundry. Hanging right inside the door was the freshly gutted carcass of a young buck, with his head hanging down and his antlers still attached.

"I don't see how you people can stand goat meat," the ranger said, looking the habeas corpus up and down "why don't you save your goats for milk?"

Up to my ears in the Seton books and determined to be a Northwoodsman even though we were only eighty miles from Mexico, I considered my grandfather's fame, as a man who'd once killed deer with a Colt .45, a challenge. My father still had the legendary weapon. I took it over, with a couple of dozen moldy cartridges, and tried to become a good shot with it—at least good enough to hit a standing deer at thirty or forty yards. I shot at a three-foot-thick pine tree a dozen times before hitting it, and by the time I was down to five shells (three had been duds) I decided to give it up, since the recoil of the big gun had made my hand sore, and besides, I lacked the money to buy enough cartridges for more practice.

The pistol continued to fascinate me, however. Still in very good condition, it was a real old Western "hogleg." I practiced fanning it like the old-timers had done, by rapidly slapping the high hammer back with the heel of one hand while aiming it and holding down the trigger with the other. Experts can make a single-action pistol go like a machine gun this way. I got pretty fast with it. And I made a holster out of an old boot top, cut way low for quick drawing. I spent a lot of time crouching, wheeling, and whipping the gun out. I was all right at the crouching and wheeling, but since the gun was heavy and the front

sight had a habit of hanging on the holster, my swift action usually ended in a frustrating anticlimax.

One evening, after practicing like that for a while, I wiped the gun carefully, loaded it with the five cartridges remaining after all the shooting at the pine tree (this left one empty chamber under the hammer), and put it on top of our old upright piano in the living room. Then I forgot the gun and started working on a one-finger rendition of "My Country, 'tis of Thee." Tiring of this piece, I picked up the music book with my right hand and started flipping the pages over until I found something new to study. I still don't know how it happened, but while holding the book in my right hand and studying it, my left strayed idly to the top of the piano, picked up the gun, and thumbed the hammer. This rotated a live cartridge into position, and the first thing I knew my ears were ringing (I don't remember hearing an explosion), the tip of my right thumbnail was clipped, my whole thumb was powdered black, the music book was somewhat mangled, a hole was ripped in a panel of the heavy oak door leading into the hall, and another hole was in the corner of the bedroom wall, where my father was sprawled on the bed reading a magazine. That gun threw a big hunk of lead.

While Sid yelled frantically from his bed on the porch and asked what had happened, Pop took a broomstick and lined up the path of the bullet, from where it had left my position at the piano, gone through the door, and into the corner. He sighted over the broomstick at the bed and made the interesting discovery that if the powder had been fresh and had driven the bullet on through the flimsy wood corner, it would have got him in the middle of the forehead. He was a little reproachful about that.

But it's a good thing he wasn't too harsh, for only a few days later I was sitting with him on the running board of our car while he cleaned a repeating shotgun, and he blasted a load of bird pellets across my nose, missing me by about two inches. That sort of made us even.

Lacking cartridges for our arsenal—which included a 12-gauge and a 410-gauge shotgun, the .30-30, a .44 pistol, and two .22's, including mine with the bent barrel—I took up archery for a while. Once again referring to the Seton books, I learned how a bow is shaped from lemonwood, osage, or yew. Lacking those woods, I did it with willows. When dry, willows are too brittle, but green ones have a lot of spring, so I made bows from the green stuff and replaced them when they dried. Since willow dries fast and shaping a bow requires a lot of carving, planing, and testing, the process ran into work. I made reasonably good arrows of tiny willow shoots, attaching rooster feathers so they'd fly straight. At first I cut arrow-heads out of tin cans, splitting each arrow and tying the points in tightly with string. But the tin heads were pretty bendable, so I took to filing points out of old pieces of iron. Since I weighed about 90 pounds, my bows were never very powerful, but it's amazing what even a weak willow bow will do. I used to put those arrows clear through the sides of wooden apple boxes.

I made so many arrows that I used up all the old feathers our single rooster had left lying around, and took to catching him and pulling fresh ones. He hated the sight of me. I'm sure it didn't hurt, because I always felt him over for loose ones which were about to drop anyway, but I know it raised hell with his pride, because he never looked like a whole rooster at any one time.

Pop became so impressed with my earnestness about

hunting and woodsmanship that he undertook to teach me how to get deer with our .30-30 rifle. He showed me about stalking upwind so the quarry couldn't smell the hunter, how to walk quietly through brush and trees, and

how to watch for game early in the morning and at dusk in the evening, along trails and at watering places. By this time Sid was up from his bed and active, but he didn't come along for the hunting lessons—he still preferred mechanics. So Pop's days were pretty well taken up between creeping around the hills with me and dismantling engines with Sid. He was very useful to us, but he didn't have much time for farming.

I never got myself a deer, despite Pop's hard work. I still had my smoking habit, and I couldn't resist lighting up when I went out hunting alone. I'd creep and crawl and stalk as I'd been told, but every once in a while a slight crashing in the brush ahead of me would show that my clouds of smoke and the reek of Bull Durham had advertised my presence to a deer as well as if I'd been clomping along and whistling at the top of my lungs. But the fresh air did me a lot of good and I never regretted the time spent on an unsuccessful hunt.

One of the books in the Seton set was a full-length novel starring a hero named Rolf who lived in the Northwoods with a wily Indian friend and trapped and sold valuable pelts to keep the wigwam full of sowbelly and beans. Now, several people in our part of the mountains had started regular fox farms and raised silver fox like rabbits, except that fox-farming is much more lucrative and much more delicate than rabbit-growing. It cost several hundred dollars for a good set of parent foxes, and a great deal more money to house the animals and buy fences and feeding apparatus. It seems the silver fox is more fragile than his red brothers, and more liable to sniffles and diseases, especially when in captivity.

Having read the book about Rolf, I went to a newly started fox farm, owned by a friend of my family's, to look at one of these fabulous beasts. The owner wouldn't let me near the pens; he said a mother fox had a new litter, each little offspring worth a fortune, and that newly

delivered matron foxes were so sensitive to noises and strangers that any emotional upset or fright would cause them to eat their babies, one to a gulp, leaving only the tips of their little silver tails.

I'm still not sure he was telling the truth. It seemed to me that if this were true, silver foxes would have become extinct long before anyone had the idea of draping them around ladies' necks. Mothers would have gulped down batches of children every time a moose sneezed or a thunderstorm came up.

A few weeks later we heard that one of our friend's foxes had dug under the fence and escaped. In our shed where we kept tools, scraps of lumber, and such auto parts as might rust in the open, hung half a dozen steel traps (coyote size), which had been there for years. Possibly they were the result of one of my brother's numerous barters.

Taking a final look at the Seton book to make sure my methods were right, I set off into the hills with the traps and a chunk of bacon. I looked for holes where a silver fox might hide and for trails where he might tour. There were far too many of these for my six traps, so I was very choosy, selecting only cozy-looking dens and well-trod animal boulevards.

My book heroes had set their traps in holes they dug deep enough so the top of the trap would be flush with the ground's surface; then they had covered the pan which springs the trigger with split bark or some such authentic material. Having only pine, piñon, and cedar bark available, none of which was suited, I had brought toilet paper.

I laid a double-folded sheet over the pan, sprinkled dirt very gently and lightly over the entire trap, scattered the fresh-dug dirt left over into the bushes, then dropped pebbles, twigs, and pine needles over the surface until the camouflage was so good you could hardly tell an amateur trapper had been messing around there.

Next, I dug a channel for the three-foot anchor chain, laid it in and covered it as I had the trap, then wired the end to the base of a scrub pine so my silver beauty would not go dragging it off. After studying the bait problem for a while, I hung a small piece of the bacon to an over-hanging branch directly above the trap. Possibly I was influenced by a mental picture of Aesop's sour-grapes fox, dancing about on its hind legs trying to reach the morsel. The bacon was pretty insecure spitted on its twig, and it occurred to me that a worthless squirrel might make off with it. So I began tying the bacon to the branch. I was so engrossed in this job that I stepped on the trap. It only stung a little, because it snapped broadside on the sole of my shoe, which was stiff enough to hold the jaws. I re-set and recamouflaged the thing, then set the other five: three more in trails and two right in front of cozy-looking holes, so the occupant couldn't miss the trap while entering or leaving.

I'd read in the Seton books and in other stories how caught animals often gnaw their legs off to escape, if left in traps too long. This seemed not only very cruel, but wasteful, so I got up quite early next morning and made the rounds of my trap line.

I had five skunks and a badger.

Now the Seton books had made several eulogies to the skunk—how he's a gentle, easily tamed, good-natured little cuss, whose tolerant humor comes from the fact that he doesn't have to be afraid of anybody. I felt criminal when I saw the first skunk standing painfully with the jaws of one of the traps I'd set on a trail clamped high on his foreleg. His tail was down and he looked very dejected. I hadn't brought a gun. I'd known I'd have to knock off the

silver fox if I caught it, but had figured on using a club or a rock so the pelt wouldn't be punctured, and it just hadn't occurred to me that I might catch anything lesser than a red fox, if not a silver one.

My first reaction was to let the skunk out of the trap, but as the abused little creature caught sight of me standing fifty feet away he hoisted his battle flag. I knew that unless I explained my intentions he would pay me back for bunging his leg up. Seton had said you could approach a skunk by speaking gently to him and moving toward him slowly. But this didn't apply to my trapped skunk. I inched up to forty feet, saying every nice thing I could think of in my gentlest tone; his flag stayed up, and I could see him checking range, windage, and drift as he sighted over his shoulder at me with one beady eye.

Regretfully, I went home and got a gun. Perhaps the ASPCA will argue that I should have held my breath, put on goggles, and gone ahead and released the animal, paying the price for having hurt him. But I didn't see it that way at the time. There were no shells for the .22, so I took the big, long old .30-30, went back, and shot the skunk. He never knew what hit him, but he sprayed the air for some seconds after death. I gingerly removed the remains from the trap, using a combination of shoe, branches, and finger tips, and got only slightly smelled up. I carried the trap on the end of a long stick, and proceeded to the next trap, and the next, finding a skunk in each. I tried to reason with them all, but they wouldn't listen.

At the fourth trap I found I'd set it in a badger's doorway. I hadn't known before that a badger could emit a musk even more penetrating and overpowering than a skunk's. Since badgers also have powerful teeth and terrible claws, it seems to me that nature overcomplemented the creature in weapons and firepower. This badger was a poor marksman; he let fly long before I was within range, and he was way to the left of target. I shot him, too, then went on to the rest of the skunks.

Skunk pelts were worth around a dollar and a half in season, and badgers two or three times that much, but I was after bigger game, and besides they had smelled themselves up, and the .30-30 bullets had ruined the pelts, so I buried them all.

By midmorning I was home with the traps dangling

from the stick. I knew removing each skunk had left its
mark on me, but only a little at a time, and after the second one I had got used to the odor. Not so my family.
I had to scrub my shoes, my hands, and all my outer cloth-

ing with kerosene. I built a fire and smoked the smell out
of the traps, then surveyed the morning's work. The rifle
shells cost eight cents apiece. That was 48 cents. A considerable portion of our pasture land was going to be un-
tenable for several weeks until the rain had washed away

the perfume. And when different people heard that I'd been trapping, they naturally wanted to know why I went after skunks at all, since I didn't take the trouble to skin them.

To answer truthfully would have been embarrassing. Our fox-farming friend wouldn't have liked to know I was after his property, and I was sure he *would* have considered it his property, although I had reasoned with myself that the fox's escape had put it in the public domain; and anyway, how could he prove it was his fox if I had caught it? He hadn't branded it, had he?

So I muttered something about "darn skunks bothering chickens" (which they did occasionally), and ended my trapping career. Some time later I learned that the refugee fox had returned to its pen a day after its escape, apparently having found life in the woods too rigorous. I also found out why professional trapping was seldom done around Mountain Park: skunks are very numerous and confident little creatures, and very curious ones, and it is impossible to set a trap in polecat country, however crudely concealed, without having it full of skunk in a very short time. Some people say you don't even need to set a trap for a skunk—just leave it in the woods, and he'll have a couple of buddies spread the jaws while he climbs in.

After learning all these facts, I was surprised to find that a boy from High Rolls, a friend of Sid's, had gone trapping about the same time I had. He came up to our house, carrying a small bottle in his hand, said he had heard of my experience, and wanted to compare notes with me. He admitted that he, too, had had the silver fox in mind, and had bagged a number of skunks.

But it turned out that he had been more resourceful than I. Deciding there must be something valuable about a woodskitty besides its pelt, the courageous fellow had actually cut the musk sacs out of his skunks with a pocketknife and had squeezed the musk into the bottle he now carried. It held about half a pint.

Sid and I agreed with our friend that a bottle of such highly concentrated horror should be useful for something. We consulted several books and by chance came across the information that musk is used in perfume manufacture because of its clinging qualities. The book didn't say what kind of musk, but we were positive that none could be so permanent, potent, or clinging as that in our bottle. We referred to it as "ours" because Sid and I felt that by coming to us for advice our friend had automatically made us his partners, and besides, we did all the book research.

We tried, without success, to find the name and address of a perfumery in the magazines and the books around the house. Then we thought of the big mail-order houses, which deal in every possible kind of merchandise. Two letters went off in the next mail. One of them read:

Montgomery Ward and Co.
Chicago Ill.
Attn Perfume Dept.

Sir,

On hand we have one half pint (½ pt.) pure fresh skunk musk. We garantee it is one hundred per % pure and not mixed with water or other objects.

We know musk is rare and nesarry in making perfume and have decided to offer this pure musk, free of foregn matter, to you because of Montgomery Ward and Co's reputation as a business that offers only the best to people.

We have also told Sears Roebuck about the musk and have decided to sell the bottle to whomever makes the best price soonest.

Yours Truly

Mt. Park Trappers, Inc.
℅ Mauldin
Box 24
Mountain Park, N. M.

The letter to Sears Roebuck said exactly the same thing, and included the same hint that if Sears didn't hurry Montgomery Ward would get the musk first. We buried the bottle in a deep hole and waited for the bidding to start.

We never got an answer from either firm. Almost every day for two weeks our High Rolls partner walked up to see if we'd heard anything, but by the end of that time he sort of lost interest in the project and in the bottle. It remained buried while Sid and I began looking around for some noncommercial use for it.

Two boys with a half pint of essence of polecat can be a real menace to humanity, and it didn't take us long to find a victim. Contract bridge had become a favorite pastime among the adult population of Mountain Park, and my folks were addicted to it. At least three nights a week one or two tables were being played in our living room. Sid and I had begun to hate the game. A kid doesn't mind going to bed at his appointed hour if he feels everybody else is tired or asleep too, or at least quiet, but it's pretty rough to lie in your bunk, trapped and forbidden to light a lamp, while sounds of vulnerable small slams and redoubles come bounding through the thin walls.

Sid and I came to pin all our hatred of bridge on one player who was frequently at our house, a hulk of a man with the voice of a hog caller. He was so loud that he couldn't even pass a hand without almost blowing his partner out of his or her chair, and when he groaned and muttered over a bust hand it shook the rafters. One night, while Sid and I were in bed suffering through a game and this big Voice was booming about how he wouldn't mind two or

three deuces every time but he didn't see why he always had
to catch all four, we heard Pop say to the fellow that the
sprouts were asleep and could he please talk a little lower,
huh?

"Ah, you can't wake kids up just by talking over a card
table, not if they've done their work and are tired," the
Voice said, making the screen door on the sleeping porch
rattle. Somehow this remark infuriated Sid and me. We got
out of bed, put on our shoes, went out and dug up our skunk
oil, and hardly whispered a word to each other all the time,
our minds were working together so well.

I was all for saturating the upholstery of the Voice's shiny
new two-door sedan, which was parked behind the house,
but Sid, with his knowledge of machinery, had a subtler
idea. Very quietly, we got the car's hood up, dipped a twig
in the awful bottle, and smeared juice on the exhaust manifold. The rough, porous metal soaked it up right away, and
when we gently clicked the hood shut again, not a whiff
of skunk could we smell. We sneaked back to bed and
popped right off to sleep.

The very next day the Voice was back to see Pop. Somehow, he'd run over a skunk on the way home from the
bridge game last night. He hadn't seen the animal, but he
sure as hell knew he'd run over one—about halfway home,
because that's when he started smelling it.

"This morning I got under the car and looked all around
to make sure the polecat wasn't hung up in the frame or
wrapped around an axle, and I didn't see a sign of it," the
Voice said, "but on the way to the store about noon, there
it was again, stinking away. Sid, I know doggone well it's

caught in the car someplace. You're pretty good with cars, and I thought maybe you could find it."

Pop didn't really like the Voice any more than Sid or I,

but the fellow was a fourth for bridge, and Pop was always obliging, even to enemies sometimes. He sniffed all around the car.

"I don't smell anything," he said, puzzled.

Sid and I just happened to be standing near by. Pop called us over and asked us if we smelled skunk. We dutifully whuffled around the machine and were able to report truthfully that we could smell nothing. Then the Voice himself nosed around.

"Well, I'll be damned," he said. "It's gone."

"Just your imagination," said Pop to the Voice. "I know how it is. You smell a skunk by the side of the road and you get to thinking about skunk and first thing you know you smell him on your clothes and in your car and every place. But it's just in your mind."

The Voice got in his car, started the engine, and drove away. He rounded the sharp bend by the apple house and disappeared, and we could hear his tires scrunch along the road below toward our gate. Just before the gate, we heard gears grind and an engine race, and in a twinkling he came backing around the bend and was with us again.

"Now smell it, damn ya, now smell it!" he roared triumphantly at us, jumping out of the car. We sniffed and sure enough there was a mighty powerful skunk odor around that automobile.

"Tryin' to tell me it was just my mind," the Voice muttered, as Pop, now really puzzled, went down on his knees and peered around the car's abdomen. He searched and searched and couldn't find a thing.

"Maybe it got flung up into the engine," Pop said. "Did you look under the hood?"

Sid and I glanced at each other. Our Pop was no dope.

There was nothing under the hood but an engine and a very strong odor. But the funny thing was that as the engine sat there dead and the hood stayed up, the odor seemed to die somewhat. Pop smacked his forehead with his hand and said to the Voice:

"I got it figured out, but you may not believe me. You hit the skunk with your front wheel and the wheel, turning fast, threw him right up in the motor. He was either dead or awful surprised and he stunk up the place before he dropped out again. You got it over your motor and you don't notice it when it's cool, but when it gets warmed up from running that juice really starts steaming."

Brilliant. Pop now lacked only one detail to complete his analysis and Sid and I felt we should withhold that.

"Isn't there anything I can do about it, Sid?" the Voice asked plaintively.

"Well, it's a new car," said Pop, "and I know how you feel about it. You might take a brush and a lot of kerosene and scrub the motor, but you'll never get it out of places like the exhaust manifold because that's cast metal and very rough and full of pores the skunk soaked. You'll just have to let the stink wear itself out. Might take a few weeks. Or you could sell the car in Alamogordo, grab the money, and run like hell before the guy you sell it to does any driving in it."

The "few weeks" estimate was way off. Far into the following cold winter that car could be seen running around with all its windows open, the Voice inside wearing a heavy coat and wrinkling his nose. Sid and I were quite callous about it; we never had any regrets, and we kept the bottle of skunk oil for months in case we should ever need it again some time.

There were two kinds of skunk around Mountain Park: the traditional, striped polecat, and a spotted type, known to connoisseurs as the "civet cat," but to us as the "hydrophobia cat." Legend had it, and we believed many legends in that country, that the civet was born with rabies, having inherited it from his parents, and carried it with him all his life, spending all his time looking for something to bite and infect.

There was a discussion about "hydrophobia cats" going on in the post office-store one day when I went over to get the mail. Several men were discussing a rumor that a fellow up beyond Cloudcroft had been nipped by a civet and was, at that moment, chained to his bedstead, snarling and foaming at the mouth—with his unhappy family around him—begging for water in his brief moments of lucidity, and then throwing a fit when it was brought to him. During one fit he had burst his chains, the sickness having endowed him with tremendous energy, and had lit out for the hills, leaving a trail of foam behind.

The whole countryside had turned out armed, according to the rumor, with instructions to shoot the unfortunate citizen on sight. Three or four of his cousins or uncles or brothers had spotted him, huddled and snarling in the brush, and by dint of great cunning and courage, risking their own lives, had subdued him and taken him back to his bedstead, where they'd fastened him with bigger chains.

How much of this tommyrot the chatterers believed, and how much they put on when they saw me standing there open-mouthed and transfixed, I don't know. But I do know I had to go out just before sunset that evening and bring in our milk cow. She had hidden herself well on one of the two heavily wooded hills of the pasture, and when I had hunted until the sun was almost gone and the shadows were getting awful long, I got old Bud, the work horse, and continued searching from his back, inspecting every clump of brush and every tree before we came abreast of it. I knew that if the rabies case had indeed escaped again and was lurking about, my chances on Bud's back were no better than they'd have been on foot, for a man powerful enough in his delirium to break out of chains would sure as hell be able to outrun poor old Bud. But it was comforting up there on that huge white back.

It was a rough night. I didn't find the cow until it had got quite dark, and when I did find her she got playful and wouldn't let me haze her home from horseback. Bud was willing, but cowpunching was one item of his education that had been neglected. I was riding bareback and guiding him around by pulling his mane, and when I had set him on a course it took a lot of tugging to change it. The result was that bossy danced around us in circles.

I'd been determined to stay on Bud, come what may, but when we got to an open space where there was no brush for several yards from which the poor rabid maniac could ambush, I got off so I could pick up a switch and get the damned cow headed right. My plan was to jump right back on Bud and keep her going. But as soon as I was afoot and occupied with the cow, Bud took off. No amount of screaming would bring him back. He was very quickly lost in the trees.

At this point I would have been perfectly willing to let

the project go and head for home, and if the cow's udder dried up from neglect, that was her own doing. But now I needed her. I figured it would be better to go home in the company of even a cow than alone. If the maniac saw or heard her crashing along through the brush, he might snarl, "Just a cow; I'm out for juicier game," and not notice the small figure trailing in her wake. Fortunately, as soon as Bud had gone the contrary cow started home in a perfectly straight line. I didn't have to drive her at all;

I just held onto her tail so I wouldn't lose her, never looking over my shoulder once during the ten-minute journey. I decided that if the menace was there it made no difference whether I saw him or not before he leapt; if I was going to get chewed up and infected with hydrophobia, I'd just as soon not complicate it by heart trouble. I was surprised to get home safely.

The scare stayed with me for days. Finally I decided that the fellow must have died, and I began to feel easier. Then a new rabies scare came up. This one was more likely based on fact. Seems that a coyote had picked up the disease on the plains near Alamogordo and had infected several of his friends, and that the pack of them had decided they might as well go nuts together. It is likely that there actually was *one* rabid coyote, but it takes much less than that to start the most spectacular rumors in some places.

So every time I heard a coyote yowling his favorite song on a hilltop at night, I was sure he was the scout for the rabid pack and was signaling that he had found our house. Nothing could get me out at night. I invented the most fantastic excuses for not going after the cow, and my Pop would get very sore, but I wouldn't move, and he'd have to go clumping angrily out with a flashlight and find bossy. I still don't feel a bit sorry about that, for I remember he was one of the many embellishers of the rumor about the rabid coyote pack.

One evening when Pop had gone cow-hunting I dug up an old magazine to find some light reading and take my mind off my terrors. The first story I found was a reprint of an old classic about a fellow who had been bitten by a dog that died of rabies shortly afterward; the man lived way out in the wilds with his pretty young wife. I couldn't have found a worse story, but I couldn't help reading it.

This poor man in the story knew he was infected and he tried all the home remedies he'd heard about from the Indians and in folklore. He slept with certain kinds of nuts and berries under his mattress; he ate certain herbs; he did everything except tell his wife. Finally one night he felt a spell coming on and knew he was doomed. He sneaked out to the shed and then far into the deep woods, and weeks later he was found dead where he'd chained himself by the foot to a tree, padlocked the chain at both ends, and thrown the keys far away so he couldn't reach them when the madness set in. Then he'd gone crazy, chewing bark off the tree and tearing up the ground in a huge circle the radius of which was the length of the chain.

One bright day while the coyote scare was on I was walking through the lower orchard when a hellish racket broke out all about me. It was a baying and a screeching and a moaning—the most blood-chilling sound I'd ever heard. With a scramble I made the upper branches of an apple tree, wishing it was a giant redwood. The coyote pack was on me! I clung to the tree with my eyes tightly shut for a moment, then looked fearfully about to see how many of the slavering beasts were attacking. I couldn't see a thing, but the horrible noise continued. I couldn't locate it—that was the most awful part. I even looked in the branches of trees, including my own. I knew then they were creeping about in the low brush patches here and there in the orchard and that they would wait all day and all night for me. So I fixed myself comfortably in a crotch of the tree and prepared to spend my life there.

As quickly as it had started the noise stopped, then started again much fainter. At that moment I just happened to look up in time to see the last echelons of an immense migration of geese go overhead, screeching and baying and moaning.

My legs were like rubber when I got to the ground, and I was so shaky it was a quarter of an hour before I could start home in a straight line.

However, some good came of the episode. After that fright I was sort of purged of morbid terrors, and it took a lot to bother me again.

The New Deal came to Mountain Park that fall, and Pop was offered a government job. It looked as if we would have a profitable apple crop for the first time, and all he needed to do was supervise the picking and selling, but that seemed a little dull to him, so he left the crop in his family's more or less capable hands and took the offer.

Pop's new job gave us the first steady income we'd had in a long time; it payed him $150 a month, which wasn't

bad money in that country during those times. He was
foreman of a crew that went about building outdoor

toilets, at a very small charge to those who could afford it, and free for those who couldn't. This is one government subsidy that was a wonderful thing—the crew ranged over hundreds of square miles, building scientific johns in scientific places. It improved the health of many communities where people had been getting mysteriously ill for years, from having their privies near and above their wells.

The crew traveled in a truck containing all their equipment, and Pop led the way in an almost-new $700 Pontiac coupe he'd bought on the installment plan for the job. Today, more than fifteen years later, the johns they built are still standing, good as new. The crew would dig a very deep pit, first making sure it wouldn't contaminate any water sources. They molded a concrete base, wide enough for one or two holes, depending on the owner's needs. The base was fitted carefully over the pit and all chinks were filled in, so there was no leakage of air. The seats were lined with smooth wood, painstakingly shaped and sandpapered down, then a tight wooden cover was hinged on. A length of galvanized pipe came up through a hole in the floor of the john and ran through the corrugated iron roof, going on up to a sufficient height to ventilate the pit without annoying passers-by.

The building itself was a fine, solid structure, made to withstand rain and wind, and the carving of ornamental half-moons or stars for ventholes was left to the owner. In some of the poorer sections, such as one tiny community of farm workers in the plains north of Ruidoso, the outhouses put the regular dwellings to shame, and people who'd never thought of painting their houses and cleaning their yards did so to prevent the government toilets from looking so conspicuously elegant.

I think Pop really enjoyed that job. It beautified the countryside, encouraged community spirit, and gave him a real sense of accomplishment, since one of his johns could be found almost anywhere. To show how he felt about his work, he even installed toilet-paper racks, for he felt it would be a sacrilege to use Sears, Roebuck or Montgomery Ward catalogues in these fine establishments. Both my grandfather's house in La Luz, and my grandmother's place in Mountain Park, got the johns, but our house didn't, because our plumbing had somehow survived the years.

Actually, Pop did a little pork-barreling in the case of my grandfather's La Luz house, for that house had perfectly good plumbing, too. But Uncle Billy, a genuine old pioneer, really preferred to be out in his tiny, well-kept orchard as much as possible, and since he'd helped conquer the West for the public's benefit and profit, nobody can deny that he was entitled to his government privy under his favorite fig tree. Besides, the government had paid him a ridiculously small wage when he was a scout for the army during the Geronimo war, and it was about time they made some of it up to him. That's how we all felt, anyway.

Pop's new job enabled him to start giving Sid and me an allowance of ten cents a week, which was quite generous, considering those were the days of two-for-a-penny candy. Sid saved his and I spent mine on Bull Durham and Duke's Mixture; the latter was the milder of the two, it seemed to me, but it didn't stretch as far. Sid helped me smoke mine.

At the same time the allowance started, Pop, who'd either recently read a book on child psychology or had decided his sons were getting a little too hefty for corporal punishment, put us on a demerit system. He kept a sheet of paper on the kitchen wall, using an indelible pencil to prevent swindling, and every time one of us sassed an elder, neglected a chore, or failed in some mission to the post office-store, we got a certain number of marks, each costing the culprit a penny from his allowance.

The indelible pencil hurt our feelings considerably. We knew how to be economical with the truth, but we seldom told our parents an out-and-out lie. So when Pop saw that the indelible pencil was wounding us by implying that we would erase a mark for a lousy penny or two, he took to using a regular pencil. Sid and I ran neck-and-neck on this sheet, he getting more marks one week, and I another, until one awful day when something happened that made Sid the only one of the two of us with any pocket money for a long time.

I had learned the trick of making a very accurate little dart by cutting the head off a big kitchen match, forcing the eye-end of a sewing needle into one end so that an inch of sharp needle stuck out, then slitting the other end crosswise, and inserting little folded squares of paper to make four vanes. I would hurl these things at flies and daddy longlegs, with intent to kill, but I never hit one; and so one day I marched up to my grandmother's house in search of bigger game. A small load of boards, for some repairs on her combination garage-and-woodshed, had arrived from Alamogordo, and with them a black widow spider. I found the spider darting around on one of the boards, tried several times to hit it with a dart, then gave up and smashed the creature with a piece of wood. I went in to tell my grandmother about my kill, and found her leaning over the sink, polishing some glasses. Without turning around, she discussed black widows with me for a while, no doubt getting them thoroughly on her mind, and then for some reason which will always be a mystery to me, for I loved my grandmother dearly, I let her have it.

She was frozen with horror for a second; I'm sure she thought the black widows had her. When rage took over, she didn't bend my ears with a stick of stovewood, as she had every right to do; she marched grimly to our house and began wearing out the pencil on the demerit chart, carefully and neatly (she wrote a small hand) making a tally-mark through each four perpendicular marks, until she had run out of paper. I counted the marks later; there were several hundred pennies—so many that I wouldn't start collecting again until I was at least two years older.

My Pop was all for making the penalty stick, but later, as my grandmother's pain wore off, she relented a bit, possibly because she figured a kid facing an allowanceless two years would see no point in ever trying to be good. She took most of the marks off, but I had to bum Duke's Mixture from Sid for a long time, and he was very tight with it.

(As should happen with all such pleasant people, my

grandmother's story has a pleasant ending. Uncle Billy's wife, a sweet and energetic person, died shortly after George Bemis's demise. Uncle Billy spent several rather lonely years puttering around his house and orchard, and Nana sat all by herself in her Mountain Park house,

sipping tea with occasional friends who dropped in. Both began to feel their years, and had they gone on that way, probably neither would be alive today.

(Evidently the same thought struck them simultaneously; she felt sorry for him and made a trip to La Luz to see how he was getting along, and it's a wonder she didn't bump into him on the road, for he was thinking of paying a call on her. My parents' marriage, which had cooled the two families toward each other, had long ceased being a subject for anger, and they found it easy to become great friends. The gallant gentleman, in his eighties, paid dignified court to the charming lady in her seventies; she accepted, sold her Mountain Park house, and the two of them have been happily and companionably married for many years. It is one of the most intelligent and agreeable unions in history. The way he holds her arm when they walk together puts young bloods to shame.)

Pop's government job ended and he came home to discover that predictions of a bumper crop in apples had come true. Pickers—single ones and whole families of them, from Oklahoma, Arkansas, Texas, and points unknown—began flooding the countryside and swarming through the trees. Dozens of trucks, some of them pulling big trailers, toiled up the mountain, bought fruit by the bushel and the ton, and hauled it away to distant markets.

In all farming communities, harvest time is marked with good cheer, for the weather is pleasant and a man can see the results of his year of hard work come in. Most farms around Mountain Park had cider presses. Kids collected bushels of windfall apples, ground them in choppers attached to the presses, and squeezed quarts of pulpy juice, which we drank on the spot or hid away in jugs and bottles in the vague hope that the stuff might become hard cider and not vinegar.

Most truckers who came to haul away the crops were independent operators. Selling a load to each one involved haggling about market prices, quality of the fruit, and margins of profit, with drivers claiming farmers' prices would hardly leave enough gain to pay for the gasoline consumed on the trip and farmers accusing truckers of making fortunes on each bushel.

I think if the supply of government privies had not become greater than the need for them and Pop's job had lasted a while longer we'd have done all right with our own crop, getting cheated a little now and then, perhaps, but ending the season with enough folding money to carry us through until another crop came in successfully. But when Pop took charge he began to get ideas.

"Why take the time and trouble to fuss around with each of those fellas separately when we could hit up a deal with one man and let him take our whole crop?" he asked us. "We settle a price with him, he hauls a load, comes back real quick and hauls another one, and we just sit back and collect from him. I was talking to a trucker today and I tells him this idea and he says that's fine, it ought to be profitable for the hauler, too. No time wasted jawing about each load."

"Too big a crop," we said. "By the time he would've hauled all those apples in just one truck half of them would be rotten and snow would be on the ground."

"Naw," he said, "for a deal like that this fella says he could get his hands on two, three trucks."

And so it was done that way. A nice-looking young trucker, the same one, I think, with whom Pop had first discussed the idea, hauled away a large part of our crop in a remarkably short time. He took only fancy eating apples, leaving several loads of culls and windfalls, good only for cider, and cooking apples, which we sold to individual truckers. As the weather began to get blustery and cold and the last load of fruit rumbled through our gate, Pop sat in the living room happily thumbing through a roll of several hundred dollars.

"That's the way to do business," he said triumphantly. "Quick and easy and profitable. Just look at these shekels, kids." Sid's and my eyes popped at the greenbacks as he riffled them and spread tens and twenties like they were cards.

"But that's chicken feed," he said, getting warmed up and pulling a check out of his pocket and waving it. "Look, this is our real money huh we can have ourselves a toot in El Paso with that chicken feed cash I was showing you and Kitten can get some new clothes huh this is real money. Just before that boy I made the deal with took his last load he says to me 'Mauldin I don't know why more people around here don't do business like you do' and I says I don't know either but it sure is simpler this way isn't it. Well I says maybe huh they'll catch on after a while and realize while it's fun to argue with a lot of truck drivers it's better to close a deal with one of them and get the business over with."

"Better cash the check," said my mother.

"No hurry huh we can take it to El Paso next week and set up a bank account with it. It's going to be damn fine to have a bank account and cut out all this chousing around the country and be just farmers and live a steady life for a change. These sprouts need it. They're getting older and ought to have a regular home and a place to bring their friends huh Kitten?"

"Sidney, you'd better cash that check."

"It's so damn funny I says to myself this morning, how we leave this place and go chousing off to homesteads and mines and projects to get ourselves some security, and right here has been our best security all the time huh. From now on we stay put and don't take a foot off this land. By God I feel good. Asthma hasn't bothered me for weeks."

When the check bounced in El Paso the next week, we had spent, luckily, only a little of the "chicken feed." On the long, unhappy, hundred-mile drive home, we realized that roll was all that stood between us and very hard times for Lord knew how many seasons. We weren't angry at Pop—you can't feel harsh toward a man who looks thoroughly crushed for the first time in his high-spirited life.

The first fifty miles we drove in silence, Pop staring dully at the road, his head sunk between his shoulders, and his hands listless on the wheel. But at sixty miles his chin came up a bit; at eighty his lower lip was pulled in tightly, and when we got home his eyes were on fire and he was muttering vehemently to himself. He hadn't said a word aloud, but my mother knew what was on his mind.

"Sidney," she said, "you can't go running off after that fellow. After all, maybe he was honest and was just hoping you wouldn't try to cash the check until he'd sold his loads and put some money in his account."

"Like hell!" Pop exploded. "The bank that damn check was written on never even heard of the whelp. He's crooked as a dog's hind leg."

"All right," she said. "We're broke again. But it's not too bad. We've been that way before. We can get along fine if we watch ourselves and cut corners. That ten dollar government check of yours just about takes care of the grocery bill, and we can grow most of the stuff we need. It's just that we can't buy a lot of new clothes and go to town so much, and we'll have to give up the Pontiac."

"I can help, Pop," said Sid. "I got five dollars cash that

crook gave me for working on his truck motor. We got *something* out of him, anyhow."

This was the supreme sacrifice for Sid. Not only was it a complete surprise to us, for we hadn't known he'd worked on the truck or that he could make money on his mechanical ability, but Sid was one of those people who always knew when somebody else had money, the while keeping his own financial status a total mystery.

But Pop wasn't even listening. He started into the bedroom.

"Sidney," his wife called desperately after him, "remember what you said only a few days ago about never leaving the place again, and how we were going to quit running off? You can't go after that man."

Pop returned, carrying Uncle Billy's old single-action Colt, and began cleaning it.

"I think that whelp lives in Corpus Christi," he said. "One of the truckers I was talking to told me. I'll bum a ride so you won't be left stranded without a car."

"Oh, Sidney, why don't you just get the law on him if you know where he lives? Why do you want to go all the way down to Corpus Christi and get yourself arrested for carrying that gun?"

"No law about carrying a gun if it isn't concealed," he said, sticking the long pistol barrel down into his hip pocket. The entire butt, including the cylinder, was exposed, and it threatened to fall out any moment.

"So long, folks," he said, and we watched him walk across the valley to the store and almost immediately catch

a ride in a pickup truck headed downhill. We knew he'd
be back.

He was. He'd forgotten the cartridges, which lay where
he'd been cleaning the gun, and besides, Pop wasn't really
a killer at heart.